PROPERTY INNOVATORS

SUCCESSFUL PROPERTY INVESTORS SHARE THEIR TOP TIPS

P
POWERHOUSE
— PUBLICATIONS —

COPYRIGHT

Powerhouse Publications
Suite 124. 94 London Road
Headington, Oxford
OX3 9FN

www.PowerhousePublishing.com

CONTENTS

"They feel like somebody actually cares, and they're not just a number... You can make a really big difference to their lives."

"A lot of the famous entrepreneurs are dyslexic. It's just the way that their brain is wired; I think that helps them do what they do."

"When I was fourteen, a teacher told my class that we would be lucky if we could become dustbin men when we grew up."

"For every pound that a client has spent on their loft, they've earned £10 back on the value increase. It's nuts."

INTRODUCTION

Have you ever thought about investing in property, but you felt daunted when you looked into it?

Maybe you've wondered how to get started and what your first steps should be.

Or perhaps you have a property portfolio already and you're looking to grow and diversify it. You'd like to know more about alternative ways of doing things. You're wondering which strategies will fit in with your lifestyle and skills, as well as giving you the best bang for your buck.

You'd like to know what other investors are doing – what has worked for them and what hasn't. What their lightbulb moments were and what has really accelerated their progress.

Whether you're a beginner to property investing or an experienced landlord, you'll benefit massively from hearing the insider secrets of other successful property experts.

What's especially exciting about this book is that it's a powerful fusion of innovation and creative thinking.

You'll therefore come across a range of specialist areas that you may never have considered before.

These include:

- luxury loft conversions

- high-rise buildings

- nursing homes

- property financing

- listed buildings

- remote investing

- housing for local authorities

In addition, there's also plenty of innovation and creativity with more traditional areas such as residential and commercial development, lettings, and management.

You'll discover exactly what these property innovators did along the way to create their success. They'll share their biggest 'aha' moments, their failures, and the achievements they're most proud of.

And the good news? If they can do it, you can too.

I hope you'll be inspired by their stories.

Cormac Thompson-Hale

Powerhouse Publications

MITUL AND GEETA PATEL

"Our business and property portfolio has been built on family values and our success is seeing our family and clients grow and prosper through property."

Job Title: Mortgage Advisers and Commercial Finance Specialists.

Personal Bio: Mitul and Geeta run a successful mortgage advisory firm, having met 24 years ago. Both have been involved in the financial world since leaving school. Mitul had been self-employed for a number of years when Geeta joined him 18 years ago, at the time their first son was born. The freedom of self-employment has allowed them to raise and spend time with their two sons (Sami and Jaimi). They have used their experience and knowledge to help their clients build portfolios and secure futures for their own families. When they are not working, their other passion is Liverpool football club and, as season ticket holders, they try to attend as many matches as possible.

Business: Lemon Tree Financial.

Services: Helping people finance their dreams and secure their future.

Awards:

UK Top 250 Mortgage Advisers 2016, as featured in *The Sunday Times*, 29 March 2016.

Best Mortgage Broker 2016, London – Wealth & Money Management Awards.

Mortgage Broker Firm of the Year (UK) 2017 – Finance Monthly Fintech Awards.

Contact:

T: 020 8723 7517

E: mpatel@lemontreefinancial.com

Website:

www.lemontreefinancial.com

♦ ♦ ♦

Mitul: My parents were immigrants; we were forced out of Uganda by the soldiers of the Idi Amin regime in 1972. I was five at the time and my brother was aged three.

This was a frightening experience for us as we left behind our home, local friends, and possessions. We came to this country with little money but we had family support. We just worked hard, like everyone else does when they come to a new country, and we progressed from there.

Growing up was tough; I suppose it was difficult for everyone but there weren't all the distractions of social media, computer games, etc, so there was more time for friends and playing in the park. It was a happy childhood but my parents were always working.

My dad used to work for London Transport and my mum was doing secretarial work. Being the eldest child, I had a lot of responsibility. I don't think children do this nowadays but at the age of seven, I wore a key around my neck and I was bringing my younger brother (who was aged five) home from school. Seeing my parents working all the time was my greatest motivation. I didn't want to do the same thing that they were doing but, even at a young age, I appreciated that they were making sacrifices for us and for a better life. We did our bit by working hard at school as my father had been a headmaster in Uganda and valued education above everything else.

Geeta: My parents came here in the late 60s, from India. They were first-generation immigrants, so they came with practically nothing and worked hard. I was born and brought up here along with my two sisters.

We lived in rented accommodation for most of my childhood and when I was 14, with the help of a housing association, we finally moved into our own home. This had been my mum's wish for such a long time: to have a place she could truly call home. My parents worked nine to five and were happy as employees but from an early age they instilled the importance of education – that it was up to us to make sure we worked hard at school so that we could progress further. My dad would always say that even if you lose everything you have, nobody can take away your education and wherever you go in the world this is what will help you in the future. This is what we have also instilled in our sons.

What was your first job?

Mitul: I graduated in accounting and finance and I learnt a very important lesson just after that. I didn't actually see myself as an accountant for the rest of my life; I enjoyed interaction with people. I worked for a couple of years in the financial planning arm of an accountancy practice, where I learned quite a lot, and then I spent another two years working as a financial advisor at NatWest (before they decided to lose their independence and become NatWest Life), where I met Geeta. Being tied to one company wasn't for me; I wanted to remain independent so I became a self-employed adviser and that's the way I've been ever since, for the past twenty-plus years. Within six to eight months of that, I bought my first property and that's where everything really started.

I had an entrepreneurial background as my dad had a wholesaler business after he left London Transport. At a very early age, my brother and I used to help in the business and we saw my dad working long hours there. We lived in Harrow and the business was in East London, so it was more than an hour's drive each way, and he usually came home after 10pm and left home at 7am, seven days a week. My father's dedication to working very long hours for his family has been a big influence on me.

Geeta: I went to work in a bank because that was considered a good career opportunity at the time and my parents always wanted us to be safe and secure. While I was working at Natwest, I met Mitul and he knew I wanted to get out of the banking environment after eight years and do something different. Mitul already had a couple of properties when I met him and he was always thinking of different ways to do things. Through him, I learned how not to always rely on a job but be more entrepreneurial. I'd been working all my life in financial services, always thinking about the safe option. He showed me a different way to do things and I've learned a lot from him over the years about the benefits of being self-employed and the difference that owning property can make. Income from property gives women choices, in particular around bringing up children and so forth.

Mitul encouraged me to leave NatWest and I went to work for Price Waterhouse, which is probably the best decision I could have made. When you're working in an environment like a bank, everything's closed in; they make you feel like you can't leave because there is only the bank's way of thinking. Until I left, I didn't realise what else was out there.

How did you buy your first property?

Mitul: It was fairly accidental. I thought I would buy a house for the future and rent it out, so it was self-financing as an investment. The plan was to convert it to a residential mortgage and move in when I eventually married. Once I had bought the first one, though, things snowballed a bit as I saw that the returns were pretty good. Obviously, this was 28 years ago, before the market really took off. We bought our first three-bed semi, then bought a second one, and a few flats after that, and so on. Initially, my parents were very cautious on my behalf because they weren't into borrowing money but they helped me out with some of the deposit. The builders did the refurb but as a family we did all the decorating and furnishing, so they were involved from the start. Then, after I bought and rented my second property, my parents weren't as cautious as they became confident in my ability. They used to pass over the local paper with the property section circled and they'd say, "Mitul, I think we should go for this property!", which was an amazing turnaround for them.

My dad enjoys DIY, so now he looks after and helps manage many of my local properties. If a gas safety engineer needs to visit, he's there, and he also supervises any building or maintenance work. He loves it, and my mum's in the background now and again to help with furnishings. Even though, initially, they were worried on my behalf, I've always had parental support. I couldn't have done it without them. Not just investment but moral support, and I felt as if I could achieve anything knowing that I always had my parents' support.

That's the type of upbringing we had. I wouldn't say I had an easy journey but sticking together helped us progress.

What were the first steps you took to build up your property portfolio – did you find it easy?

Mitul: Because I was in the industry as a financial advisor, arranging mortgages and so on, the scariest step was the finance as I'd only been working less than a year. It was scary borrowing money after being a student, especially because my parents weren't 100% behind me at that stage. But I worked out the figures before I bought the property and I knew I could make it work. The main problem we had was that there were no buy-to-let mortgages, as such; the phrase was only invented about fifteen years ago and this was twenty-eight years ago. There were only two or three lenders that did so-called investment home loans, whereby they would offer you a residential rate with a premium on top of one or two per cent. But as I was in the industry, I could research those lenders that would consider investment home loans and that's how we progressed, leveraging the portfolio. At the same time, I also helped to start building my brother's portfolio. Fast forward to the present and his current portfolio allows his wife the financial freedom not to work.

I met Geeta when we were working together in the bank and we got together a little bit after that. I had about four or five properties at that point; however, the portfolio took off after we got married, with our joint incomes and savings. It also helped that we lived with my parents for the first two years of our marriage, so we could save for more deposits.

Geeta: Mitul's help gave me confidence. Before I met Mitul, my sister and I had bought a studio flat but we didn't have any advice, so we just bought what we could afford. It was our first investment and it wasn't one of the best investments we ever made as we ended up with negative equity. I was a bit afraid of property, given that experience. But what I learnt, from being with Mitul, was that we hadn't had proper guidance when we bought it. If you're a new investor, somebody will tell you how to get a mortgage but nobody takes the time to advise you on how you should invest, where you should invest, and what you should be looking out for in an investment property and I think that's where the pitfalls are.

We bought a new-build property which had a high service charge and problems with the tenants not paying rent and all sorts of things that you don't realise when you buy, and this was not making us any money. That's where Mitul's help really came in handy in managing the tenants and expenses. Eventually, he helped us sell that property and I saw that if you do something properly, it works. His properties weren't expensive but the location was right, his tenant profile was right, the price was right. Being with Mitul was on-the-job learning. I thought, "Hang on, he's really good!" We got married and we knew we wanted to start a family. I really didn't want to go back to work once we had children. So together, we were able to grow our property portfolio to a point that I would not need to return to work. That's what the income from property gave us: flexibility and freedom of choice. We got into it, we enjoyed it, and it was something we could do together and see the benefits and the fruits of our labour.

Mitul: People knew that we had property because I didn't make a secret of it but we never pushed it out there and asked people to invest with us or anything like that. It was our own journey. When we first started – in fact, until about fifteen or sixteen years ago – I don't think people really realised how buy-to-let investments could improve their lives. Our friends and family didn't fully understand buying properties for investment. It wasn't in the press; it wasn't in the papers every day or on TV as it is now; nevertheless, we just got on with it. It's only in the last fifteen years that people have realised we have a portfolio and that's because I discuss it if clients ask me what I would do myself when they get into property. Once people realised this is what we did, they would come to us for advice because we've been there, done it, and got the t-shirt.

What are the benefits of being a husband and wife team?

Mitul: As we are both working towards the same goal, it is easier to work together. We bring complementary qualities to both Lemon Tree Financial and our property business, which allows us to progress with relatively few disagreements. There are no office politics; we trust each other and we have a strong sense of family from our upbringing. By working hard and long hours as a team, we believe that both our lives and our children's will be easier in the future. Although we still have stress in our lives, working together allows us to understand each other and work through the stressful times together. The bottom line is that it is give and take for the greater good, which makes us stronger as a couple.

What have your challenges been along the way?

Mitul: I think raising finance has been the biggest challenge as there weren't lenders around who wanted to lend to us. Other challenges come just from being a landlord. We have done a lot of decorating, sourcing materials, finding the right team around us, looking after tenants, and building relationships over time. We've been lucky in that we have never had to take anyone to court in 28 years from a portfolio of 44 properties.

We started buying local to us in Harrow before we moved out of London to look at properties with better yield. Most of my tenants have been there five or ten years. In fact, my oldest tenant has been there eighteen years. They will not move until I buy a bigger property that they want to move into, so we would like to think that we've done something right with the tenants. We try to appreciate that although it's a business to us, the tenants regard it as their home. We respect their time and space, keep them updated on what's happening, give them feedback, and if there are maintenance issues, we try and act either the same day or within 24 hours. So, the tenants know that we always look after their interests. Consequently, they think we're pretty good landlords – not the type who just sit back and wait a week before they action anything.

Geeta: We've realised over the years that it's about the people; it's not about the property and the money. We treat the people around us right – and that's not just the tenants, it's the team that works for us and the builders that come in. We've got a good relationship with everybody. The builder that we have coming around is almost like family; we can give him a set of keys and the work will be done. That's come with experience over time.

Mitul: One of the biggest challenges that we had in building the portfolio in the early stages was the interest rates. I first started buying the properties during the recession and interest rates went to 15%. Yet the figures still worked out at the time, but it is always important to understand your income, expenses, and the bottom line.

How did Lemon Tree Financial come about and what do you do today?

Geeta: Our original company name was M and G Consulting. But a few years down the line, we had a call from M and G Investments, saying, "You're using our name." Even though we had nothing to do with them, we didn't advertise or anything, we had to change our name. We were doing some brainstorming; we wanted something different because financial advisors usually use their names. Mitul thought of Lemon Tree Financial. People still comment on it, so we must have got something right.

Lemon Tree was born out of our desire to work together to build a business on honesty and integrity, where we could help others with our knowledge and take the stress out of buying a home or investment properties. This also gave us the freedom to raise our sons and spend quality time with them.

We haven't looked back since then, really. We just find it easy to work together. I knew what office politics were like and I have none of that. Self-employment can be hard work and long hours but you really don't mind it when you're working for yourself because you know what the end goal is. You know what you're working towards whereas, when you're employed, you're working for somebody else.

How do you differ from standard mortgage brokers?

Mitul: We can be judged on the clients that come back to us year in, year out. Most of our mortgage and protection clients have been with us for fifteen or twenty years. So, I believe we differ from other brokers first and foremost because we try and really understand the client. We ask them why they are doing what they are doing and what they would like to see happen. The client understands that someone's listening and has empathy with them. They know we are a broker who will always do our best to get them closer to their goals by researching different solutions from a 'bird's eye view'.

We basically help the client from the initial phone call onwards. At the initial meeting, we explain about mortgages, the costs of buying a property, and the potential pitfalls if it's a buy-to-let property and we help them from that point until they find the property. Sometimes we act as a sounding board for investment projects because not only are we advisors but we have investment properties ourselves and the clients ask us what we think. Unlike other brokers, there are many times when I tell a client that this particular property won't work and say, "I don't think you should go for it", even though we get paid for arranging mortgages. For example, if there's some due diligence that the client hadn't checked, I would point them back to the agent and explain why they should check things further. If everything checks out, great. If it doesn't, I'll explain where the pitfalls might be.

From our personal experiences, we know where things can work and where things can go wrong, so any new client has the benefit of that experience and knows that we'll try to keep them on the straight and narrow. So, really, we offer them time and advice before they find a property, during the process, and, sometimes, even afterwards. We willingly share our personal experience on the property side because the clients are our lifeblood. That's how I like to think that we differ from other brokers as we help clients build their portfolios as well as their confidence.

We also have 200 or more genuine testimonials of how they fared with us, what we did for them, and how we helped change their lives. That keeps us going because we know we've done a good job but, also, when people can put up any review they like, and one bad review can potentially damage your business, we do our best to make sure that we always manage expectations and help our clients out.

In summary, our service is focused on the client's needs, empathy with the client and good communication throughout. As a result of our service and dedication, our clients are loyal and many have been with us as long as 20 years.

Geeta: By acting as their trusted adviser, holding their hands throughout the whole process. From start to finish, even before they've found a property, it's understanding what our clients need. Because sometimes, we need to tell people that what they're doing is not the right thing for them. We'll deal with the buyers and even the sellers. I had a case a couple of years back where I had to keep the seller happy because our client, who was the buyer, didn't have all the finances set up. We kept up good relations with the seller just to make sure that everything went through. We even advise them what to say to the estate agents and we liaise with agents to keep them updated. Literally, we work with our clients from start to finish as we know the property-buying journey from our own experience. As we've had problems ourselves, or seen other people having them, we can take that stress away and make sure that, for our clients, it's a smooth journey.

What are the success stories that stand out for you?

Mitul: Our client testimonials tell the story behind our success and we believe it is our tenacity and the attention to service that we provide which delivers the results. We deal with landlords and individuals who are first-time buyers, right up to one of our landlords who owns over 200 properties. For example, a couple of years back, we had some clients with credit issues. They were Londoners trying to buy their first buy-to-let property in Liverpool. They didn't even own their own property and it was a struggle for six or eight months to get their credit issues sorted out first and then they bought their first property. To this day, I can remember the phone call I received when they got their keys. The wife was on the phone: "Whoo-whoo!" To hear that excitement and know we'd helped these young people start off on their property journey was great. She actually said to me, "I'm calling you before I call my mum." To this day, I remember that, and thinking, "You know, it's a nice thing we did." Things like that keep us going. Three years later, with our help, they have three buy-to-let properties now as well as their own residential home.

Then, a couple of years ago, we had a client who'd completed a property course. She was a high-flyer in the City but had decided to leave her job and concentrate on property. She'd been to other brokers, who said, "Well, sorry, we can't assist you, because you don't have the income." But she had assets, and what we always try to do is ask enough information to get an overview of the client. So long as we know what the client wants and what their position is, we try to come up with solutions. So even though all the brokers she'd been to before said she couldn't do it, she now has three investment properties and she's on the second development of a 16-bed HMO. She's enjoying going on holiday every few months. But to some extent, her success is a joint thing – us helping her has made her pretty successful. We get referrals from her because she understands what we are able to do. We didn't just say no; we looked at her situation and found a solution. She's not gone back to work; now all her income is from property and she is happy being out of the rat race.

Another scenario was when we had a single mother with two grown-up lads. She'd separated from her husband and wanted to start in property investment. She'd done a property course and wanted to get further. She had very little capital but, again, we looked at the overview of her position. The property she owned was still with her ex-husband who had not lived there for over five years. We were able to raise finance on her home and buy out her ex-husband with the help of her sons speaking to him. So, after we showed her the way to move forward, she now has two investment properties; she's on a different path and much happier and she understands that property is going to help her sons out. At the same time, she's coming up to retirement, she now owns her property in her own right and she's moved on from the challenges of divorce to having two investment properties. If we can help a real person with real issues, that's what I call a success story.

There are many more success stories and many clients have shown their gratitude by posting honest reviews about how we have helped them. We even had a poem written for us by a client.

What are the lightbulb moments in your property journey?

Geeta: One was: avoid doing things we don't normally do. We took our focus off Lemon Tree and decided to invest in a nightclub. It was a joint venture with another partner and we were spending a lot of time, energy, and money on it because it was meant to be extra passive income for us. But it didn't turn out quite like that. It's an industry that we didn't really know much about and it's not as straightforward as financial services or property. I think we soon realised that this wasn't going to be how we had intended. So, we took the decision that we were just going to run it to a point where we could sell it on as a going concern and then move out of it.

At that point, when we took that decision to sell, we were able to put our focus back on property and we realised this was what we knew well and what we should be focused on and we haven't looked back since.

Mitul: Essentially, that 'aha' moment for us was: if you're going to build a property portfolio for yourself, just focus on your goals because everything else is noise and will divert you from your overall goal. Everyone has different property strategies but you know your goal: you know the financial freedom figure that you are looking to achieve and what your timeframes are.

Do everything you can to get a step closer to your goal rather than divert to other strategies or other projects, which would delay your progress. From then on, you can focus your mind on things improving going forward.

Potential lightbulb moments often come about whenever we meet lending managers and the like and we learn of new criteria and products because our first idea is, "Ah, I know how this can help clients." But I think the biggest realisation is just the understanding that you should always give value.

Always try to help others first and you'll be looked after one way or another; that's what I firmly believe.

Geeta: The biggest realisation for me is looking at my children and appreciating that I have been able to spend quality time with them from the moment they were born to now – and the oldest is going to be eighteen in a couple of weeks. The income meant we were able to send them to a private school but it was more about being able to be there – to pick them up from school, have dinner together, and so on – which we could never have done if we were working outside the home and didn't have that additional income from property. Now, both our boys are at that age where they'll be looking to go to university. They have respect for people around them: their peers, their teachers. They're doing well at school, not just in terms of grades but being well respected as people. They're grounded individuals and I think that's because we were able to be there for them. Property gives you choices. Even now, they'll come back to us and if they've got a problem, we're there to talk through it with them. As a mum, that's a big thing for me.

What are the top mistakes you see with property investment?

Mitul: I would say it's fine to have the dream and to chase the dream but you have to understand what property allows you to do. It's a matter of focus. Understand your why and your passion; try not to get too distracted by other things as that's one of the biggest mistakes I see with clients (I have been there myself).

Also, I often see clients who have gone on property courses or learnt things on the Internet. All education is great; it's how you apply it that counts and sometimes the best advice is just to use your common sense. For example, one of the most important things I mention to clients is that it's not always possible to reduce an asking price by, say, 25% or 30% straight away. It just doesn't happen like that. You've got to remember there's a human being selling that house and, in a way, you're disrespecting them by making an offer so low. There should always be 'give and take' and a good feeling going forward, rather than lots and lots of rejections because you've put in offers 25% below the market value. You not only turn off the vendors but you could also turn off a lot of agents who can see you coming and think, "Ah, they're just going to offer ridiculous amounts." What clients forget is that the agent is not working for you; the agent is working for the vendor. They get the best price for the vendor and you have to remember that.

Another thing that I come across with a lot of clients is not wanting to 'leave money in the deals', as they say. I tell them that we should look at that before refinancing. I point out they need to doublecheck the cost of refinancing, the valuations, the legal costs, penalties they will incur, and so forth, as well as checking that in the local area comparable prices are higher. Otherwise, remortgaging is just not cost effective. Given where we are in the market cycle, we're finding surveyors are much more cautious, so even if a client believes that they've bought a property, done some work to it, and can pull out money, the bottom line is that it's the lenders' surveyors who decide on the value. We try to manage expectations but there are a lot of unhappy clients who find out the property's valued at less than they thought. Therefore, it's not always possible to recycle all the money.

One other mistake that we advise clients about when it comes to mortgages, whether for residential or buy-to-let or investment property, is to avoid too much credit card debt because lenders are beginning to take a much tougher stance on what they deem as lifestyle debt. Mortgages can be declined – even buy-to-let mortgages – if lenders feel that you're not running your own personal liabilities well enough.

What are your top tips for newcomers to property, people at the beginning of their journey?

Geeta: I think first-time buyers are always really keen to get started straight away. Which is good because it's very positive but sometimes we have to slow them down a little so they think it through more, take it step by step, and understand why they're doing it. Sometimes they just tell us, "It's a really good deal! I have to go for it!" and they're scared of missing out if they don't take the leap. We always say, "Put it on paper. Work it out because that costs nothing." Then they feed it back to us and we go through it with them to check whether the numbers work out and whether they've made the right decision. That's where we come in, as a sounding board. Newcomers need that.

Mitul: One of the best tips we've discovered for building a successful property portfolio, and any business, is developing trusted connections. It's all about people and it's always best to build connections at an early stage in the particular area that you're looking to invest in, such as a good letting agent and reliable builders. Your 'power team' should include a good accountant so that you set up your portfolio as tax-effectively as possible, a solicitor who has been recommended to you and who gets the transactions through as quickly as possible, and a good mortgage advisor who is not just experienced in the market but is a property investor in their own right, so they can help you leverage things going forward. Essentially, build a team around you and it will help you be successful because a lot of investors are now buying outside their own areas and it's not easy travelling 50 or 100 miles to your property every time there's an issue. Get a good team you can trust and leave it to them. Look after them; their business is your business. Treat them nicely and, on the whole, they will look after your properties and you'll have peace of mind.

Research is very important. It is really important to understand your target rental market by speaking to agents or doing due diligence online. We sometimes have clients who say they want to set up an HMO or a multi-let in such and such an area but they don't actually know if it will work there. It might be a family area where they don't appreciate HMOs or multi-lets. Or maybe it's an area where there's no local employment, so an HMO won't work. We've had people who want to do student lets because it's a student town but the property's a good half an hour from the university.

If you don't know your target rental market, you're not going to be successful.

Learn to be an effective delegator. Basically, this means knowing how to work with other people and matching the right person with the appropriate task. By understanding the relative strengths and weaknesses of your team, you play to everyone's strengths.

Just to finish, although property has its benefits, you should always look at the money you put in. Once you've done all the research and got your facts and figures, check it's still a good investment or whether there are other areas you could put your money to work better for you. Just because somebody says that a property is the best thing since sliced bread doesn't necessarily mean it's true – make sure that your money is actually working for you. Do the maths on each and every project before you offer on it.

Don't make the mistake of making an offer on a property when you haven't done the figures properly and then trying to backtrack on your offer. It doesn't really work with agents.

What are your biggest achievements?

Mitul: My biggest success or achievement is related to the fact that this is a family business and property has allowed me the financial freedom to help my family. My father, unfortunately, had a heart attack over eighteen years ago and it took him about seven months to recover enough to go back to work. Luckily, I'd built enough of a portfolio that I was able to let my father retire. I basically told my dad, "You're not going back to work. We have enough income to support you." He had some pension income as well a few years later, so for the last eighteen years, my father's been happily retired. He's had to do some DIY at some of my properties but he loves that anyway. My parents have made sacrifices for me and being able to do that for my dad was our biggest achievement. I retired my mum the following year, again, because of our property. She liked the social aspect of work but I saw that she was tired and I said, "Mum, leave it. We've got the income. You don't have to worry about anything."

People dream about cash flow but I firmly believe the important thing is what you do with that cash flow. I wouldn't have changed anything for the world.

My parents are still fighting fit now, going to the gym every day, having a full life. I have gone some way to repay them for all the sacrifices that they made for myself and my brother after being thrown out of Uganda.

Equally, because property has given us financial freedom, we've been able to give our two sons a good start in life in terms of education but, more importantly, spending more time with them. Because we're self-employed, we are able to work around our two boys and spend a lot of time together. We still pick them up from school, so I know the ins and outs of what's happening there, and we have time with them when they come home before they start their homework. We always have dinner together as a family. Recently, my two boys have been able to buy their first investment property using their savings from Christmas and birthday presents and a top-up from the grandparents and us. We bought the property in trust for them but they're actively involved and it's their own project. They live and breathe property and they know about the running expenses, the mortgages, how everything works, so it's basically making them self-sufficient. It's taught them things that maybe the school isn't always able to do – finance, budgeting, and dealing with people.

They help us with property accounts, they help us when tenants move out; they've seen what property can do for them and they both said, "Well, we want to do something." It's making use of their money going forward: they bought themselves a golden goose that's now going to lay the golden egg – the rental – for the foreseeable future. I would like to think they've got their heads screwed on and will be successful in their own right. My older son, for example, has decided to go to university. When I asked him, "What do you want to do in life?", his words were, "I'm going to go to university but in the end, I don't want to work for anyone, I want to be self-employed like you, Dad." He's got the entrepreneurial spirit, and I was really pleased when he said that. Both boys will always have that support because of what we've been able to build up over time.

After graduating so many years ago, I am lucky enough to be working in an area which I am passionate about.

Geeta: For me, it was always important to be there for my sons because I see so many mums go out to work. I met up with some mums last week and most of them are back at full-time work now and they were talking about their relationships with their teenagers. They're finding it so difficult because they can't talk to them. I sat there quietly because I didn't want to say, "Well, actually, it's fine for me." They just come home, and they tell us, "Mum, do you know so and so...this is happening with so and so." I don't have to drag it out of them because they know we're not going to judge them and we're here to support them. We want to make sure that they don't miss out on anything in terms of taking the opportunities and risks they can at this age, which we didn't do because we were cautious at that age. We've always said to them, "Choose a subject that you enjoy." We're hoping that when they do finish university, they'll be doing something they enjoy from the beginning, unlike a lot of clients that we see. So many people hate their jobs; we've met three accountants who hate their jobs in the last few months, so they want to invest in property to get out. We want to avoid that for our kids.

A few years ago, a teacher client wrote a testimonial for us starting with the quote "No one who achieves success does so without the help of others" (Alfred North Whitehead).

Lemon Tree Financial and our support team have many years of combined experience in the mortgage and protection market and have been together for over 18 years. Having the benefit of knowing each other personally for a number of years (almost like family), working in a relaxed home office, where we all have a knowledge of what our clients' needs and goals are, helps to ensure that at no time will one individual staff member feel that they were not included in our overall achievements. Our staff have helped us achieve awards such as:

UK Top 250 Mortgage Advisers 2016, as featured in *The Sunday Times*, 29 March 2016.

Best Mortgage Broker 2016, London – Wealth & Money Management Awards.

Mortgage Broker Firm of the Year (UK) 2017 – Finance Monthly Fintech Awards.

What kind of people have you helped over the years?

Mitul: Over the last 28 years, we've worked with over a thousand clients, including first-time buyer landlords, property developers, and portfolio landlords with up to 200 properties. We've helped generations – from the initial clients, we're now helping their kids. It's been important to us that we've been able to help our clients progress in life and build their portfolios from nothing. I think two or three of the clients have now decided they're financially free and don't need to work anymore. It's just a great feeling when you're able to help a client see a different way forward. We have been invited to countless dinners and lunches and so on because everyone's so grateful for what we've been able to do for them.

The other side of our being able to help is that we have financial freedom. Although I don't always have the time to work for charitable causes, we do contribute to charities which range from children's charities, Cancer Research, and LFC Foundation. One very important thing that we taught our boys, from a very early age, was that whatever monies they receive, be it Christmas, birthdays, Saturday jobs, they will always give 10% to charitable causes. We've also taught them that if you can't give money, you give your time, which is equally important. And financial freedom has helped us help other clients with their own charitable causes.

Geeta: When we take a client on board, it becomes personal to us. Whatever their challenges, we will approach them as if they are our own. That's second nature for us; we don't even think first. If someone comes to us with a challenge, we will find a way and if there isn't a way, it really upsets us but that happens quite rarely. Sometimes it's a case of we can't do it right now but you need to do this, this, and this and then we'll revisit in three months' time. On the whole, we have been able to help a lot of people sort themselves out financially and get them on the path to having a happy and successful life, which is what we're aiming for. For us, it's a really good feeling when we help somebody. I don't think you can really put that into words or quantify it. It just feels good. The day we can't help anybody is the day we stop because that's the part we really enjoy.

Mitul: People remember what you've done for them and that doesn't usually happen in transactional business like being a mortgage broker. Maya Angelou said something along the lines that people will forget what you said, people will forget what you did but they won't forget how you made them *feel*.

ADAM McCORD

"People can make things look really complicated and difficult – but I was just a standard guy that saw that there was an opportunity to earn some more money by renting out some rooms."

Job Title: HMO Specialist and Director of ADM Property Group.

Personal Bio: Leaving the corporate world after 10 years and going a totally different direction to his upbringing, Adam mastered the ways to maximise profits from property to enable him and his family to be financially free. Adam now owns a multi-million-pound HMO portfolio, all managed by the company he founded. Adam now focuses his attention on growing the portfolio and helping others who are considering making HMO investment a success.

Business: ADM Property Group Ltd.

Services: Property Training and HMO Management.

Contact:

T: 02392 988441

E: adam@adammccord.co.uk

or hello@admpropertygroup.co.uk

Website:

www.admpropertygroup.co.uk

♦ ♦ ♦

My upbringing was pretty unique. My dad had a job as a computer consultant travelling the world. It might sound nice and glamorous but in fact it's a lot of being in very loud airports, dingy hotels, being away from friends and family, and eating in restaurants by yourself.

He was working long hours and I would go for weeks sometimes without seeing him at all. That went on for a couple of years until I was nearly 10. He was literally all over the world for weeks on end and then he finally got a placement in Zurich, Switzerland. When he came home, my mum would say, "Where are you going next week?" He would reply, "I've got to go back to Switzerland." And this went on and on. He said to his bosses, "You seem to keep wanting me to go out to Switzerland. Do you want me to stay for a bit longer? I'd like to arrange for my family to come over if it's for a serious amount of time." And they confessed, "Okay, cards on the table, we want you to be there for a year."

Me and my mum packed up our bags and moved there; we didn't speak one word of German. I got put in a foreigners' school where they concentrated on German for pretty much your whole day. Once you became fluent in German, they allowed you to go to a normal Swiss school. On my 11th birthday, I took a cake in with a knife so I could share it with my classmates. Literally, as soon as the teacher walked out of the room, one of the kids picked up the knife and I narrowly avoided getting stabbed straight through the stomach. Unfortunately, I was in a class with people that were coming from war-torn countries, with bombs going off all the time, and it seemed violence was the only way that they could express their feelings. Strangely enough, I didn't like being in that school with all the bullying.

As soon as I had that knife turned on me, I decided the only way to get out of that hellhole was to learn German. So, I learned German pretty rapidly. A little after my 12th birthday, I had just settled in my final Swiss school and my dad said, "I'm going to send you back to England, with your mum, so you can go to a big school. I'm just going to commute to Switzerland for four months: I'm going to leave at four o'clock on a Monday morning and I'll come back on Friday evening, so I'll still get to spend the weekends with you." I said, "Okay, you've got to do what you've got to do."

It became a bit of running joke, because it got to the 1st January and my dad was starting to pack up his suitcase, ready to go back to Switzerland, and my mum said, "Hang on, I thought you'd finished?" "Oh yeah, they've asked me to go back out again." Then it got extended but he said, "Don't worry, I'm going to come back at the end of this year." And then the following year, again, he said, "I'm going to be back at the end of this year." As it turned out, there was no job option for my dad back in England. In the end, he didn't move back from Switzerland for 21 years!

I didn't have the most standard teenage years. My mum had really bad eyesight and had to go in for an eye operation. She was already blind in one eye from an operation that went wrong as a child so she was really fearful of having this operation done. She went in to have the operation on her good eye, the only one that she could see out of, and the operation went wrong and she was left with an infection in her eye and no vision. I had to grow up very quickly as my dad was in Switzerland. I was doing the weekly shop for myself. I was arranging to get to school and back. I was, to all intents and purposes, self-sufficient at the age of 13. What really killed me was going to see my mum in hospital and her saying, "Oh, that's a nice green t-shirt you're wearing." I walked out and burst into tears because I was wearing a red t-shirt. She was just trying to make small talk to be kind.

Eventually, her eye did get better because my dad got in contact with the consultant who did the operation. He basically took out a part of her eye and then put a prosthetic part in but she was told, "Sorry, you can never fly again because of the build-up of pressure. You can't go to see your husband." My dad would fly back to England on a Friday evening, then get in the car with my mum the next day to drive 650 miles so that she could then spend a week or two in Switzerland. Then he would drive back over to England over a weekend to take my mum home and then fly back to Switzerland the next day. It was a pretty tough time.

My dad spoke to worldwide ocular surgeons and aviation specialists for a second opinion and they said my mum should be okay to fly. They started with a short flight to Jersey. After they tested this, they gradually built up the length of the flights bit by bit to get her confidence back. Luckily, she can now fly again. My mum is a fighter, bless her.

I got my first job when I was about 14 or 15. It was working as a restaurant runner, for £2.50 per hour. I used to do an eight-hour shift to get my £20. I got a few tips, but it knackered me out, so six months later I stopped doing that.

I was keenly into computers and software programming and hardware: I started getting into developing websites. My dad kept on talking about the Y2K Millennium bug and people getting really scared. I started up a limited company at the age of 16 after seeking legal advice. I started up @lanta Consultants Limited – it was the first company in the UK in the year 2000 to have the commercial @ sign in the name of the company. Interestingly, it was only that year that they allowed you to put the commercial @ sign in your company name and very shortly after they stopped allowing it because they found out that a lot of the systems couldn't accept it – for example, getting a debit card with your company name embossed in the plastic.

I did computer consultancy and website design, and I was making a decent amount of money out of doing that, but my studies were not going too well. I went from being an A-grade and B-grade student to barely scraping by. You could quite clearly see where my attention was: it wasn't school or college, it was about making money.

My dad had a frank conversation with me when I was nearly 17. He said, "Look, I know you could probably live by yourself and support yourself but while you live under my roof, you need to be getting better grades than you're actually getting. You need to either shut down your company and focus on studies or you need to get the hell out of my house." I was shocked: I thought he'd be really happy I was making money but his point was that I was making money at the expense of my education. I thought, "Well, money is nice to have but relationships and family are more important." In a heartbeat, I closed the company down and just concentrated on my studies. I ended up with a first-class honours degree – I was one of only five people in the whole year to get one. If I'd focussed elsewhere instead of heeding my dad's advice, I don't think I would have got that degree.

What did you do after university?

As soon as I finished university, I got a job with a multinational blue-chip organisation. Even though I had a computing degree, I went into their finance department. I didn't like the job; it was a means to an end. My parents were living in Switzerland but they had a house just outside Portsmouth and I would live there all the time. Every now and again, they would come back but I always yearned to have my own foot on the property ladder. I started looking around even though there wasn't any urgency. They weren't kicking me out or anything like that, it was just more of a desire. Even as a kid, one of my favourite games was Monopoly and I used to build Lego houses.

So, I started looking around two-bedroom apartments in nice areas just outside Portsmouth and very quickly realised that with a flat's leasehold, I had to pay management and service charges. However, if I went a bit further into town, I could buy a three-bedroom house that was freehold. It would be a bigger house and I wouldn't have all these monthly bills to pay. Brilliant!

I ended up making an offer on a house and it got accepted. You could say that I started off as an accidental landlord because the first house I bought was a three-bedroom townhouse in Portsmouth. Before I moved in, I completely ripped the whole house apart. I ripped out the kitchen, I ripped out the bathroom, I moved walls, I put in rooms, I converted the garage. At the end of it, I had a very high-spec four-bedroom house. We had ceiling-mounted speakers everywhere, filtered water on tap, an 11-foot-wide projection TV, and so on.

It was my first house and I wanted to make it as good as it could be, so that's what I did. The next week or so, I was walking around thinking, "Wow, this is amazing." Then, as the weeks went on, I thought, "Actually, I'm quite lonely." When I was at university, I was living with other people in a house share. Now, I was clattering around in this big house on my own. I didn't have a girlfriend, kids, or anybody to look after, so it was just me.

As it was a three-storey townhouse, I decided to have the master bedroom upstairs with its own ensuite and then the rest of the top floor would be my office as well. The whole middle floor, with a bathroom and two bedrooms, was completely empty. I had bills and they were actually quite expensive. I thought, "Wouldn't it be great if I could replicate a sort of house share but with only people I like in it?" That was my goal: to put people that I liked into the house to help with paying the mortgage.

There were no courses on HMOs – people weren't doing it as a strategy. I started to rent out two of the rooms to lodgers.

As soon as the first rent payment came in, I thought, "Wow, I've just earned the equivalent of 50% of monthly wages after tax from working full-time with my employer. This is really good."

A few months later, the house next door but one came up for sale on Rightmove. It was a repossession. On the first viewing, I thought, "Great, I'll have this, thank you very much." I bought it. I thought, "I'm going to do what I've already done as that seemed to work. But instead of only renting out two rooms, I'll be able to rent four because I'm not going to be there. This is going to be even better." So I did that.

Then I thought, "Wow, hang on, this is turning into a career. You never intended being a landlord or a developer. Your plan was to go to college, get a job, and work up the corporate ladder. If you continue with that plan, you will get a tiny little pay raise each year, maybe a couple of per cent if you're lucky. If you kiss some real big butts in the company, you might move up a bit quicker. But you're not going to be able to double your salary every year or anything like that." It was this revelation that made me think, "I can do this again and replicate the results I got on the first property. In fact, I can probably even do it better because the first house was such a high spec that I spent loads of money on extra tech and gear that was unnecessary for a rented property."

It was only four months after I had finished my own house. I was thinking, "Shit, I want to buy this house but I don't have any money. How am I going to do this?" I put the offer in and I had no real concept of how I was going to do it. Luckily, I got one of the last 90% loan-to-value mortgages at the time, back in 2008. Now that my house had gone up in value, I was able to draw some equity out of it to put down as a deposit for this house. The day that it completed, it was all over Sky News: housing markets had crashed, everybody was pulling out, doom and gloom. My mum asked, "Are you sure you've done the right thing because it looks like a really bad idea?" I did briefly wonder if I'd bitten off more than I could chew. But I knew that the mainstream media will tell you one version of what's happening in the world; it tends to be quite biased. I kept that in mind and I thought, "Unless anything forces my hand, I'm just going to continue with my plan." So, I renovated the house then got it rented out.

In the meantime, I probably had one of the lowest times in my life. I had just finished doing a four-month refurb on my own house before I chucked myself in at the deep end again. Most people buy a standard buy-to-let flat as their first investment purchase but I was buying a standard, three-bed residential house and turning it into a high-spec HMO with no real experience, no mentors, and no guidance.

I thought, "I am my target market. If I can do things I like, then there's a high chance that people like me will want to live there." I priced it at what I thought was reasonable, rather than a scientific calculation. I didn't even look at the market. The second house seriously took it out of me as I was still working full-time. I was doing 40-plus hours at work and travelling about 15 to 20 hours a week to get to work and see clients and customers.

I was also having to do all the planning, budgeting, and talking to tradespeople and having to go out to DIY stores because I was trying to keep costs to a minimum.

I was doing over 100 hours a week of work. I wasn't sleeping much. I was also trying to see friends and family.

I had a breakdown. One day, I just woke up and thought, "No, I don't even want to get out of my bed. I can't be bothered to do anything." For me, that was the first time I'd ever experienced it and that lasted for a solid week; I didn't interact with anybody. The house that was being renovated was only two doors down, so I could see it from my bedroom window. I could see the builders working and they were phoning me up, asking, "What should we do about this?" or "We found such and such." And I didn't want to deal with it at all, even though I was geographically so close to everything that was going on.

I then pulled myself out of it and decided, "I need some kind of quality of life. I never intended to be a landlord, this is an accident. With everything that's going on with the economy, I think I might have made a wrong decision." So, I made a conscious decision to just concentrate on my career. When I came to retirement, the houses would be my little pension plan.

Eighteen months went by. I was very low and subdued and then I started to feel a bit better. I'd been keeping an eye on this one house that was only a couple of miles away. It had been on the market for as long as I'd been ill and I just wondering, "Why is nobody taking this property? If I wanted to, I could just buy it. I'm going to have to find out some more information about it." The price had gradually been reduced to offers in excess of £180,000 for a four-bedroom house in quite a desirable area of town, with a garage as well. I had a viewing and asked the agent, "It's been on the market for over a year, why can't you sell it?" He replied, "The owner went away, chucked us the keys, and told us to sell his house. He's just come back and gone absolutely apeshit because we haven't sold his house. But we couldn't get a hold of him to put forward any of the offers, so that's why it hasn't happened. He wants me to shift it." I went back to him with an offer of £130,000. The agent said, "There's no way in a million years he will go for that." It wasn't even a cash offer, just a mortgage offer. I was expecting him to just point-blank refuse and ask me to reoffer.

Instead, the agent came back, saying, "The lowest he'll go is £137,500." The market value was £180,000, so I bought it and that reignited my fire. I'd had my own house with lodgers in for about 18 months. I'd also had another rental property and I'd been working full-time, so I'd managed to save enough money for the deposit. I'd just started to build a bit of money and then here I was spending it again. I was in a sticky situation because I now had no money to do the renovations.

My parents weren't in a position at the time to lend me any money: I wasn't born with a silver spoon in my mouth and I haven't got a trust fund I can just call upon.

What I decided to do was take the income that I'd received from my properties and speak to my accountant and do a tax return. He said, "You know, on paper, this is how much extra in addition to your wages that you've earned." I then went to my mortgage company with that information and I said, "Is there any chance, now I'm earning a lot more money, that you could maybe give me some money from the equity of my house?" And pretty much to the penny, they gave me the exact amount of money I needed to do the renovations on this other house so I was able to do the refurb.

I thought, "Seriously now, Adam, this needs to stop. You only got this because it was such an amazing deal." Then, randomly, a couple of months later, two houses down my same road came up for sale and I thought, "Oh, they're cheaper than I bought my houses for. Crap! This housing market malarkey is for real. In a sense, I've lost £20,000 or £30,000 on each of those houses I've bought because of how the property market's gone. God! But if I could turn back the hands of time, would I still have bought them?" And the answer was, "Yes."

They were £30,000 cheaper than I'd paid for my house and they were diagonally opposite. I had a look at both of them and thought, "They're alright but they need quite a lot of work doing to them." I decided to put in an offer on one of them. It was up for £145,000 and I put in a cheeky offer for £135,000.

It was all going through swimmingly and then I had radio silence from the estate agents. Even that early in my career, I knew was not a good sign. As it turned out, the seller ended up having to pull out for personal reasons.

In the meantime, he'd been talking to the estate agent and found out that I wanted to convert the property into a HMO. He decided to take it off the market and turn it into a HMO himself. I thought, "Oh my God, this is direct competition and it's down my own road. This is the worst thing that could have happened." Anyway, I saw the renovation happening and nobody moved in.

A couple more months went by and still nothing happened. Then, I got a knock on my door at eight o'clock on a Sunday morning. The guy said, "You don't know me but you were looking at buying my house four months ago. I've now renovated it. Are you still interested in buying it? I've put new flooring in, I've put on new doors, I've done this, I've done that." I thought, "Wow, brilliant. I'm definitely not going to get away with my £135,000 offer because he's spent quite a bit of money." I asked how much he was looking for and he said, "How about £125,000?" I've never turned around and shaken somebody's hand so quickly! I told him, "It's a deal."

It was already a four-bedroom house when I went in and he'd done a bit of a Bob the Builder renovation. I had to redo some of the things but I wasn't really bothered because I'd got it £10,000 cheaper than I was originally happy with and it was now in a better condition.

By this point, I was thinking, "Bloody hell, I'm now earning way more than my salary." I'd managed to give myself an over 150% pay rise. Once the renovations were done and the tenants were in, it was a case of just dealing with issues as and when they came. Having four properties in very close vicinity to each other consumed about 40 to 60 hours a week, every single week, just like a job does. It was bringing in more money than I was earning from my full-time job. Nonetheless, it was handy being full-time employed when it came to mortgage applications. Around the same time as I bought this house, one of my really good friends said, "My friend Rachael's got a problem. She's living with her ex-partner, needs to move out, and wants some property advice. Can you have a chat with her, to see what her options are? You seem to know a lot about property." I wouldn't have called myself an expert at that point but I thought if I could impart some knowledge, that would be better than nothing. As it turned out, our meeting ended up being our first date and ever since then, seven years ago, we've been inseparable.

My life completely changed at that moment. I had been doing 100-odd hours a week, trying to be a Jack of all trades, and I just didn't have any time. When I met Rachael, I fell head over heels in love. When we first started going out, I never let on to her how busy I was. I was just acting like everything was nice and easy going and I could take everything in my stride but beneath the surface, I was working at warp-speed to try and make sure that everything was done. I was working really late into the night at full speed, with multiple computers going at the same time doing different things. Just literally, any minute of time that I could claw back, I had to. At the time, Rachael was still living with her ex-partner, so we were both very keen to get her out of that situation. So, I helped her get a property.

Rachael moved into a property, everything was happy days – and then I got a phone call from my dad. He said, "I'm back in England, can you come tomorrow morning and have a chat?" My dad's normally quite a chipper, upbeat kind of guy but he sounded a bit scared or nervous. I couldn't quite work it out.

The next day was a really cold April morning and as I walked down the stairs to their front door, this really weird shiver came over me. After an hour or so of beating around the bush, my dad said to me, "I've just received my annuity statement from my pension company and it's pretty grim reading. I've been paying in for years and years and years and I'm only six years away from retiring. I'm looking at this and there's absolutely no way I can afford to live on the annuity. I can't even afford to pay for our food and all the basic house bills, let alone a mortgage, running cars, having any holidays, nothing. I'm really scared." It was hideous. My dad has always been my hero. He'd worked so hard all his life and made sure that if I ever needed anything, he'd always pay for it. I was concerned about getting into a load of debt to go to university but he was really keen for me to go so he kindly paid. All the time I was at university, that was all money that was coming out of what he'd saved up. I felt really bad because my dad was working a lot of hours and doing a shitload of travelling and at the end of the month, he had more outgoings than he had incomings. Now my dad was in such a sticky financial position that my parents were thinking about selling the house and reconsidering what they would do with their life. That really upset me.

My dad said, "I've seen what you're doing with houses, I was wondering if there's any way we could work together?" I thought, "Wow, I'm really flattered but my God, what a scary responsibility. I need to sort it out because otherwise they are going to have a really bad quality of life." I just felt really bad.

I had been bleeding my money dry every single time I'd been buying my houses, borrowing the money from here and there, then saving up a bit and then putting it with some other borrowed money. I was wondering how on earth we would do this.

We worked out a plan and bought a house together, then converted it into an HMO. I thought, "Hang on, I'm going to have to share this money with my parents because we've agreed a 50/50 split. I don't want to do all of this work to only get £100 a month each. So, let's put in some more people." By the end of it, we had a six-bedroom house.

If you can create additional rooms out of the same physical asset, it means you can get more rent from those additional rooms: it's simple maths. We did that and my dad said, "Oh my God, I'm in a hell of a lot better position. You've managed to make you and ME the equivalent of what my annuity was going to be paying on a monthly basis with just one house."

My dad always used to say, "All big problems are broken up into small problems. Just take little bits and then you won't have a problem."

So, I applied the same methodology. I said, "I wasn't planning on making you a multi-millionaire by buying one house and turning it into HMO. But what we can do is this, that, and the other to enable us to buy another property."

So, we bought another property and turned that into a five-bedroom house. Then, we bought another property and turned that into another five-bedroom house. For us, it was not only about maximising the amount of profit, it was about giving people a good quality of living accommodation as well. We refurbished and renovated every single house so that it was all new: there were no Artex walls, dodgy electrics, old boilers, or anything like that.

Over the next couple of years, we bought more houses together. In addition, I also brokered a couple more property deals for my dad and he bought two apartments. One of them had been sold four years before for £150,000 and I'd managed to negotiate it down to £82,000 – a massive deal. That gave me my first taste of being a deal sourcer and negotiator in property as well. Then, he said, "I don't want to put all my eggs in one basket. We've got quite a few HMOs together, I've now got some flats but what I really want is to have is just a standard single-family house and rent it out for a reliable income. I don't want the hassle or the headaches."

At the time, Rachael and I had been discussing moving in together but I was a bit nervous about buying a house together because we hadn't been together very long. As soon as my dad asked me to find him a house and a family that would be suitable, I said, "I've already got a perfect family. But you might need to spend some money on renovations."

To all intents and purposes, we've managed to move into a house that was absolutely perfect for us, done to our own spec. Obviously, I was concerned that we were making this place our home so we agreed to do a lease option on it, where I have the option and opportunity to buy it at a discounted rate if I want to.

I've done a bit of deal sourcing and I also do training nowadays and I have some mentees. We host training groups every couple of months, as well as talking about all the pros and the cons of doing HMOs or other types of strategies. My speciality is HMOs, so that's the one that I focus on.

Typically, we do find that a lot of people who come to the courses are new to doing HMOs or property investments in general. I always tell people the good things and the not-so-good things about doing what I do. I do find a lot of property gurus are very one-sided on things. I always believe in being honest and ethical and to be forewarned is to be forearmed.

How did it feel when you finally left your full-time job?

I managed to survive 10 years and you know what they gave me for achieving 10 years of solid service? They gave me a pen! I had spent so much of my personal time, and so many hours that I wasn't being paid for, making the company millions and millions. I was a little pissed off.

Since then, I've managed full time in property. I don't work for anybody else, I own a company that does property management and training. I've got a great little team that does quite a lot of the day-to-day stuff for the business, which means I can now step away from some of the more mundane, boring jobs. Life is a lot more relaxed now. I'm fortunate to be in this position. If I want to do something, I can do it, financially and timewise. Likewise, if I don't want to do something, I have a great team around me that can fit in those things that maybe I'm not so good at or I don't want to do.

What about your lightbulb moments?

The first one was when I bought my first home and thought, "Hang on, if I rent out these two rooms, that money will pay for my mortgage. Then all I have to do is pay for the house bills and it's actually cheaper than living in student digs."

The second lightbulb moment was after the lodgers had moved in and everything was going swimmingly. I thought, "Let's roll it out: let's do what I've just done on a slightly bigger scale."

People can make some things look really complicated and difficult but, at the end of the day, I was just a standard guy that saw that there was an opportunity to earn some more money by renting out some rooms. I then decided to magnify that.

You would have thought I'd have twigged this sooner but it wasn't really until I tried to help my parents that I thought, "Hang on, if I put *more* rooms in, I can get a lot more money." That was a delayed lightbulb moment.

We like our houses to be a sort of a home away from home. We have similar age people, similar professions, a similar demographic in the property, and we also have a very rigorous vetting process for tenants.

Somebody might look really good on paper but if they've got an attitude or we get a bad vibe, we won't rent to them. Because we believe that if you have issues before they even become a tenant – if they're rude, arrogant, or back-chatting – then what the hell are they going to be like as housemates?

Or how are they going to react if we have to tell them to stop smoking in the house because it's against the rules?

Another lightbulb moment was to make sure you get some help from whoever has the correct skills.

There's no way you're going to build a multi-million-pound business as a one-man band.

Anybody that offers help, accept it, welcome it, embrace it. You shouldn't and can't do everything by yourself and you have to accept graciously the help of others.

What are you proudest of?

The thing I'm most proud of was what I did for my parents. I was only 22 when I started out, so I had another 40 or 50 years to recoup if things hadn't worked out.

But my parents were so close to retirement age that it wasn't even a case of sink or swim. It was just: swim, you have to. It scared the crap out of me doing it.

About a year ago, my dad pulled me aside and said, "I've just checked the bank balance. I just want to say thanks ever so much for everything you've done. There's absolutely no way I'd be in this position if it wasn't for you." That has got to be the proudest moment of my life.

It was a great way to pay my parents back for everything they had done for me over the years.

I don't think anything else in my property career could ever come anywhere close to that. My dad tapping me on shoulder, looking me in the eye, and saying, "Thanks so much. I don't need to worry about money now."

What advice would you give for anyone else that wants to follow in your footsteps?

You've got to have a plan *and* you've got to take action. It's one thing having a plan, but then not taking action means you're not going to be any further forward.

Look at people you aspire to be like: people that are inspirational and motivational, people that have done what you want to achieve.

Then emulate them, copy them. You're not going to get 100% exactly what they got but you will get pretty close if you follow what they've done. There will be ups and downs and there will be things you won't see coming when you're looking through your rose-tinted glasses. You will have good days and you will have bad days.

I'm very fortunate now to be able to live the life that I do and I wouldn't change it for the world.

It hasn't always been like this and you're going to have struggles. As happy as I am on a daily basis, you can't be in a constant state of positivity and happiness because that's not reality. Bad things happen, bad days happen. Accept it, deal with it. Look for the silver lining; look for the positive messages it can bring.

To take action, you've got to know what you want to do. Find somebody who can help you along the way, whether it be watching a YouTube video or going to a seminar or a mentor. You need to find somebody that's done it before because otherwise you won't have a clue what to do and you'll be running around in circles.

OLIVER MASON

"I started off as a child of two to a single mother growing up on a council estate — but look where I am today!"

Job Title: Co-Founder and Acquisitions Director, Magna Group.

Personal Bio: I lead the global acquisitions and financing team: we have been successful in acquiring and executing many land and property development projects. We have raised multi-million pounds' worth of capital from investors both within the UK and abroad. I oversee the appraisal process of individual acquisitions to ensure the risk/return ratio meets the company standards and match it to individual investors' needs.

Business: Magna Assets Management.

Services: Magna Group is a residential and mixed-use property developer specialising in transforming old buildings into stylish, high-quality residential apartments and pioneering new-build schemes in and around London. It has plans in the near future to expand internationally.

We currently have 400 apartments in construction and 350 exciting new residential schemes in planning in prime commuter belt locations.

Contact:

E: contact@magnagroup.co.uk.

T: 020 7887 6162

Website:

www.magnagroup.co.uk

◆ ◆ ◆

I went through school not really knowing what vocation I wanted to get into but I was always really interested in film and media. I loved films; I used to watch films all the time. One of my big dreams was to get into directing films, like Quentin Tarantino, so I decided, after school, to study film and media at college. But it didn't quite pan out as I hoped: I got bored after the first term and then dropped out and started labouring.

My mum said to me, "Well, I'm not going to keep you at home. You've got to go out and make some money. I think the best thing you can do is go and work with your hands and get on the building sites." So, that's what I did, though it wasn't quite what I wanted to do.

It was not such a disappointment at the time because I was still relatively young, with aspirations of getting to Hollywood. But I got into being on a building site and enjoyed it. I learnt how to do a hard day's work, which was good. Also, when you work on a building site, your boss is generally quite tough, so it almost turned me into a man in a way: I went on the building site a boy and left a man.

To be honest, I was a bit of a Jack the lad when I was younger. I was always a relatively intelligent kid but I got in with the wrong crowd.

I didn't do too well in my GCSEs. I got in trouble with the police a number of times doing things I shouldn't have been doing. I think it was just a result of the people I was hanging around with and the sort of life I was brought into, really. But I was quite lucky because my sister was about six years older than me, so she tried to take me out of that environment.

She used to travel on business doing fashion, so she would take me away with her to places like Barcelona and other nice cities to show me that there was another way, and I wasn't just stuck in the council estate and that area. I was quite lucky in that respect.

Eventually, I set up a construction company with a friend of mine when I was about 20.

For me, starting a business was the ultimate thing.

So, my business partner Chris Madelin (the CEO of the company) and I started a construction business when I was 20 and he was about 24. We were doing anything that we could do, really: landscaping, building works, building garages, driveways, patios, turfing.

We learnt on the job, so we were reading books about how to build houses and so on at night and then going and building them during the day in order to get to where we wanted to be. Then we were also doing a bit of rubbish clearance as well. We were a bit like the Del Boy and Rodney of the building trade: doing anything and everything to move forward. But it was good because we were hustlers and we enjoyed what we were doing. It was two good mates working together; it was a good thing.

What initially made you decide to set up a business?

We grew up in the same town and we used to hang around when we were little. That's pretty much how we knew each other. But we met up at a local gym when we were older and got talking again and realised we were both doing similar work, so it made sense to start a business together.

I think for me, it was the fear of not achieving that was pushing me forward in the beginning. Because I came from the council estate and a lot of my friends that I grew up with were either in prison or on drugs or worse, I was trying to get away from that. So that's what motivated me in the beginning. I was pushing away, thinking, "Right. I don't want to end up like this. I've got to get away. I've got to make something of myself." That's what really drove me forward in the beginning.

I was never that confident. People will say to me, "Oh, but you always seemed confident." Inside, I wasn't, so I was forever overcoming that internally.

How did Magna Group come about?

We were working together initially for about six years, though this wasn't under the Magna brand. We were just self-employed. We then started buying properties: we were doing them up and renting them out for an income. We got bored of that pretty quickly because it wasn't getting us where we wanted to be so we started buying land and getting planning permission. We did this with a few small sites and then we did one site that made us a nice £100,000 on the turn. This made us think, "Hold on a minute, we're onto something here. This is a lot better than being builders." So, we then decided to set up a proper company doing property development and land and planning. We knew that we wanted to create a brand because, over the years of working on building sites, we'd been listening to and reading books from entrepreneurs such as Richard Branson and James Caan. We knew that we needed a brand and we knew that we wanted to build a serious business. That's why we came up with Magna and branded it up properly while we were going along the journey. So that was the inception of Magna.

How did you feel at the start of your career path?

At the beginning, it felt like I was faking it and was going to be found out. One hundred percent. I think that's natural in the beginning. When you're starting something new and you're starting to talk to people about it and get your name out there, you think, "I haven't done this before." You always have that fear of failure and fear of people finding out that you're not who you say you are but that you're just a builder or whatever. I was trying to raise millions of pounds for deals, so in the beginning you get that kind of feeling but then you get used to it and it becomes a way of life. Your confidence grows as you achieve more things.

You do high-rise construction along with redevelopment and offices-to-residential conversions. What is your business like day to day?

Nowadays, probably 50% of our portfolio of projects is permitted developments: office-to-residential conversions. We've got a mixed bag of really easy internal fit-outs to more complicated complete strip-back to the concrete frame, adding floors on top and re-cladding, which is obviously a lot more work.

Then we have two high-rise projects, one that is in planning at the minute for a 17-floor tower and one that's just got planning for a 12-floor tower that we're about to get on site with.

We always aspired to build iconic buildings, so, obviously, tall buildings really interested us. We've got into the bones of it on the planning side and we're now just going through the construction phase on a few high-rise projects. It's something we really enjoy doing.

At the minute, we're just doing the West London commuter belt. We're not actually in London – we're in Surrey, Hampshire, Berkshire, and a few other Home Counties' territories and we're also branching out further afield.

We've got about six projects on the go. I think we've got about 400 flats in construction and another 350 in planning.

How do you cope with having so many projects on the go at the same time?

We've got a good team around us; that helps, and we just love what we do as well. We work a lot. It's our entire life. Chris and I don't really have any hobbies, apart from my family – we're just 100% focused on the business. So, although it may sound a lot, when you've got a good team around you and you're focused, it's quite achievable.

What are the main differences between high-rise construction and a standard low-level construction?

There are quite a few different methods of construction. We're going through quite a change at the moment in the way that we build things but that's still at a pretty early stage. When it comes to high-rise generally, it's a concrete frame clad in either bricks or panels. So, it's actually a lot simpler than you think and it's all done through contractors as well, so we, effectively, just put the project together.

We find the land, we get the planning, we assemble the project team, then they'll go and find a suitable contractor to come and build it. We've got Sir Robert McAlpine looking at one of our sites. We've got Osborne, which is a big contractor in the South-East. They'll come and do the actual build and we just kind of manage the process. Then, we will either manage or sell the units on at the end, so I would say it's not that complicated.

What sort of challenges have you faced over the years?

There are challenges pretty much every day. That's part of the fun. I think the issue with property is that it's a very reactive game. You've got a lot of moving parts and you're also contending with the economy and political matters that happen, such as Brexit, so there are lots of different factors affecting your assumptions and your numbers on a daily basis.

Obviously, trying to find sites at the minute is quite tough because of the sheer lack of supply of land in the UK. The demand is very high and there's a lot of competition. Then, as you move through, you've got to contend with a very arduous planning process in the UK. Although the government are saying that they're going to make it easier, and it is getting easier in certain towns and boroughs, it's still quite a long process you have to deal with and it can be very stressful. Then you've got the construction side of things, which is inherently quite risky not just from an actual build–ability point of view but from an economic point of view as well. For example, I've seen construction prices go up at least 20% because of Brexit. We've had to deal with that as well and factor that in.

The availability of contractors is also a challenge. Because there's so much building going on, there aren't enough contractors to build everything, so they end up putting up their prices and then there can be some issues there. We're dealing with these types of challenges on a daily basis: it just becomes part of the job, really, and you just get on with it.

What have your lightbulb moments been over the years? When have you thought, "Oh gosh, if I'd known this years ago?"

I think that for us it was some of the ways we financed projects in the early days. It was probably not the way we should have done it. We went in with banks with too high interest rates and it ended up costing us too much on the interest and took a little bit too long. So, I think, being able to creatively finance projects in the early days – like using options subject to planning, then trying to get all your planning as quickly as possible.

There were a few schemes where we bought unconditionally and then we worked up the planning, and by the time we'd added all the planning value, the interest rate had eaten a considerable chunk of that value that we'd added. We effectively ended up working for the banks and investors.

I wish I'd learned earlier how to negotiate and delay contracts; also, how to just structure the project team as well. We kind of felt our way through that in the beginning. We had a contractor go bust on us on one of our first projects, which wasn't good as it left us with a bit of a black hole in the project but we had added so much value through planning that we were okay, so it's important to make sure you factor these things in. But we learned a lot from that and we now work with really good quantity surveyors who go out and help us find the best contractors. And we've got contractors that we work with on a long-term basis as well, that have good balance sheets.

What are your tips for dealing with builders or coping with stress on a day-to-day basis?

The best way to cope with stress, and see yourself through all the inevitable problems, is to have a big vision and a goal. Your vision could be small, such as, "I'm going to go and buy 30 houses." So, when you come up against those problems, you're going to be more determined.

Your other goal could just be to seek out people who have done it. When we started out, we didn't know anyone who had done exactly what we were doing and we didn't have anyone to show us the way. We look back now and think, "Wow, if we had had someone who had our knowledge now mentoring us, we would have shortcutted loads of problems."

So, I definitely recommend seeking out people that have been there and done it and getting their advice. There are lots of good people out there who are professionals. A lot of people think they have to deal with builders and contractors themselves but, actually, there are plenty of quantity surveyors and project managers that are Royal Institution of Chartered Surveyors (RICS) qualified who can help you with that. They can also navigate you through the problems but you will still have to kiss a few frogs to find the good ones.

We don't have an official mentor ourselves but we've got a lot of peers that we look to. There are people in the industry that we are quite friendly with who we consult on a weekly basis. I'm constantly reading: I've got an Audible account so I'm always listening to new stuff. I'm always keeping abreast of what's going on: reading trade magazines and making sure that I'm up to date knowledge-wise on everything I'm doing.

What is the big vision that keeps you going?

Our vision for the company is to grow Magna into a global, integrated, property services business. That means having global projects – hotels, property development, private rented deals – all over the world. We don't want to be confined to the UK. Then, also having integrated services, so getting into property management and all the related services so we can be a turn-key operator, effectively.

We're already looking at some hotel opportunities abroad, so we'd like to have a chain of global hotels. We envisage having other residential and commercial developments across the globe as well. There are some economies that are going to double over the next 25 to 50 years – places like China, India, Indonesia, Mexico. So, trying to foresee where the next boom is going to be and then trying to ride that wave on the way up and build our brand at the same time.

What is unique about Magna Group compared to other similar firms? What is it that makes people come to you?

I think it's the product that we create and our professionalism as well. We hold ourselves to a really high standard – not just internally, with what we do in the business, but also with the product that we create.

Every time that we look at a deal or any project at all, it's always of the highest quality. One of the unique selling points on our Magna Homes brand is 'affordable luxury'. You can go and buy one of our flats in, say, Godalming. It's only 17 apartments but each one has got fully marble-tiled bathrooms, Neff appliances, hardwood floors, underfloor heating, wired-in Sonos speakers, and so on – so you're buying a luxury lifestyle but you're paying not too much of a price for it.

What are you proudest of achieving over the years?

I like creating things, so I'm really proud of a lot of the projects that we've done. What we are doing is creating places for people to live in, which I think is quite a great thing to do. I'm also proud of building a team and building a business that you can see running every day: it's given all these people that we employ work, adding to the economy.

I'm just enjoying every day of it, really; every day is a new day. I try to stay inspired and motivated, even after the toughest days, so I'm always reading books, I'm always furthering my knowledge in my sector and other sectors as well. I like to keep things fresh and moving forward.

What are the things that really stand out for you over the course of the career?

I think it's mainly how far I've come. I'm sitting here today in Mayfair, overlooking Bruton Street, with all the big names – with Canali and some really posh brands. But the reality is, I started off as a child of two to a single mother growing up on a council estate – but look where I am today! The main thing that stands out is how far I've come. It wasn't the worst council estate in the world but I grew up with the wrong crowd. I did everything that a young lad probably shouldn't do when growing up in that environment. So, I think it's actually just that.

It's being able to look back and see how far I've come and how my peer group has changed: the people that I have conversations with on a daily basis and the things I'm talking about now, compared to where I was even five or six years ago. I have to pinch myself sometimes. It obviously makes you proud but I keep my feet on the ground and I keep moving forward.

What has been the key to your success over the years?

I think it is never giving up and keeping a really positive attitude. Obviously, it's not easy – nothing worth having is ever easy. The key is to stay positive and be able to move forward and see problems objectively. At the end of the day, I always keep in the back of my mind that life's short and as long as I wake up in the morning and I'm breathing, then everything's pretty good from there.

As long as I'm healthy and my family is healthy, that's all that matters; anything else is a bonus. So, when a big problem arises and it feels like it's the end of the world, you look at it and think, "Actually, it's not a major problem," and you take a breather and then hit it head-on.

What advice do you have for anyone else wanting to achieve your level of success?

I think with regards to getting to be where you want to be, it's really about writing down your goals and working out where you want to get to. It's never one-size-fits-all, so you've got to really understand what it is that you want for yourself. You've only got one life, so you might as well live it and there's no point in doing something you don't want to do.

If I didn't like what I'm doing today, I would change what I'm doing. If I didn't like where I was living, I'd move.

A lot of people get stuck and they get into a kind of rhythm and I think it's important to keep taking stock of where you are and keep adjusting your course. Always hold on to the thought, "Where do I want to be in the next five years or the next ten years?" as well as "Who do I want to be?" Then build your life around that.

TUSHAR SHAH & MEHUL SHAH

"The question we ask all our staff is, 'Would you want your mum and dad to be treated this way?' If it's yes, then do it."

Job Title: Directors and Co-Founders of Centrum Group Corporation Ltd.

Personal Bio: Creative and passionate entrepreneurs who enjoy developing new businesses and teams. Started and developed six businesses in the last 12 years.

Business: Centrum Group Corporation Ltd.

Services:

Centrum Care Homes:

Residential and nursing care homes in the UK.

Development of new care homes.

Leasing and operational management of homes.

Bluebird Care:

Domiciliary care, learning disabilities, physical disabilities, supported living, live-in care, brain injury, mental health, palliative care.

Centrum Property Management Ltd:

Investment in residential and commercial property in London, Berkshire, and West Midlands.

Blenheim & Chester Developments Ltd:

Acquisition, development, and sale of residential and commercial property in London, Berkshire, West Midlands, Buckinghamshire, and Oxfordshire.

Awards:

2017: 'Outstanding': Care Quality Commission (Bluebird Reading and Wokingham branch – for being well-led and caring.)

2015: Great British Care Awards: Registered Care Manager, finalist.

2015: Great British Care Awards: Best Newcomer x 2, finalist.

2015: Great British Care Awards: Dementia Carer, finalist.

2015: Great British Care Awards: Supported Living Carer, finalist.

2011: Bluebird Care South Franchise Award.

2010: British Care Awards: National Dementia Carer of the Year Award.

2010: National Bluebird Care Franchise Award: Runner Up.

2009: National Bluebird Care Franchise Award: Runner Up.

Contact:

E: info@centrumgroup.co.uk

T: 0118 907 6598

Websites:

www.centrumproperty.co.uk

www.centrumcarehomes.co.uk

www.blenheimchester.co.uk

www.bluebirdcare.co.uk

◆ ◆ ◆

Tushar: We had very similar and very different childhoods, in a way. I grew up in Birmingham as part of a large extended family. There were about 28 of us spread across three terraced houses next door to each other.

My family came over from East Africa in the 1970s and we started off with a little shop that grew into a large supermarket and then diversified into a plastic bag factory. Because we had a family business, my mum and dad were working all hours, so I had a very independent childhood. It was lovely but also, being part of an extended family, I wasn't lonely because I always had my cousins and everyone to play with. So, it was a fun childhood but it was also a very interesting one in that I had to learn to make my own decisions and become self-sufficient from a very young age, including looking after my younger sister and brother. It was a good childhood: yes, we didn't have the money and we didn't have the holidays but we found ways of making money through newspaper rounds or in other innovative ways.

Mehul: I was born in Kenya and we moved over in the early 1980s. My mum was a teacher and my dad was an engineer but when we came over in the 1980s, it was very hard to get jobs so they would pretty much take any job that would pay the bills. They came from a background where it was all about working hard, making sure you got a good education, having the security of income, and saving every penny that you have. We didn't really have the luxuries of going on holiday and things like that. My parents' deal was: get a good education, get a good job, and you can then enjoy your life.

It was a different mindset to how a lot of people think now in terms of making sure you enjoy life and live each moment, every day.

I think one of the key points was when I got my first job and I got a bonus. I wanted to buy a property because I could see a few people around me doing that and investing in property. But my parents said, "Well, why do you want to buy a property? You don't want the headache of tenants; they'll trash the place. Look at your cousin who bought a place, he's had such a hard time with it." This is when I was about 22 years old, so, at that point, I didn't invest in property because I was led by my parents' view. For the next four or five years, I continued working in the city with the mindset of "Just work as hard as you can and save as much as you can."

During my childhood, we moved around quite a bit, so I went to four different schools while growing up. It was good in one way because I'd meet lots of different people but we were never settled until we finally went to secondary school and I stayed there for the whole period of my secondary education.

I was very close to my family, like Tushar. So, we'd spend a lot of our time with our families on holidays and events like that.

What were your first jobs like?

Tushar: My first proper job was at the age of 17; I got a Saturday job in Next, working in retail. If people meet me now, they find me someone who is very confident and is able to easily give talks and presentations. But as a child, I was quiet and reserved, purely because I was the youngest out of the cousins around my age. There are three of us and I was the youngest one, so I was always the one that remained quite shy. But when I got my job at Next, it brought out the skills that I actually had a flair for: sales and presenting and influencing people. So, that sort of set me up for my career: whenever I would be in a sales or marketing role, I really excelled. If you put me in a financial or an operational role, you're setting up for me to fail. When I look back, now, I think my time at Next and various other retail outlets really gave me a good grounding in sales, teaching me about talking to and influencing people.

Mehul: My first job was straight after my GCSEs; I started working at John Lewis. Looking back, John Lewis's values and their customer service resonates with a lot of the ways we do things now. John Lewis is a partnership and they very much look after their staff. Like us, they make sure to provide good value and information for customers. It wasn't about making the sales; it was about giving them information. If you give them good information, they'll come and buy from you, even if it is £5 more than anywhere else. So, Tushar and I have looked at our businesses in a similar way. We don't want to be the Tesco of the world, we want to be the Waitrose, where people come to us not because of the price but because of the quality and experience that they're going to receive. I think that sort of analogy really helps our staff understand the way we want to provide our service.

That was my first job and I still look back and think that was one of the best jobs I ever had because I think it really allowed me to grow out of my shell and gain a lot of confidence in speaking to people on the shop floor and it was quite a fast-paced environment, especially on busy Saturdays. So, it gave me a good grounding and taught me the value of money. I really valued that experience so early on.

I then went on to work in corporate finance and private equity. I worked at KPMG and various other banks in the city.

How did you get started in property?

Tushar: Mehul's my brother-in-law. I married his sister, so it was "buy one, get one free"! I think I got the best deal: I got a beautiful wife, who is very intelligent, but I also got a very intelligent and complementary brother-in-law, which makes a great team in business.

Our background was that both of us went to university. I studied law and then went on to do a Master's in business and Mehul did economics. We then both went into the corporate world. I worked at Mars, the confectionary group, in a variety of roles but ended up predominantly in marketing looking after all European and global advertising relationships. Mehul worked at KPMG in Corporate Finance before moving to work in investment banking.

Even though we started off in the corporate world, we both wanted to go into business. This was at time of The Apprentice (which had just started on TV) and Dragons' Den. Effectively, I grew up in a very entrepreneurial family where the family started businesses and Mehul was also very interested in business as well. At that time, about 2004, the NHS had long waiting lists and I'd helped Mars look at IT outsourcing in India.

They also have a huge medical infrastructure in India and one of the ideas that we came up with was outsourcing medical treatment. We started a company called 'The Medical Tourism Company'. That was quite innovative at the time and we set up a website; we were doing Google Ad's pay-per-clicks for one pence per click at that time. We set that up with one of our uncles, who was a GP, and, essentially, we facilitated people who couldn't afford private treatment in the UK, as well as places like the USA, to go to places like India, Thailand, and Eastern Europe for medical treatment. This varied from dental treatment and knee surgery to heart bypass. That was our first business and I think we spent a couple of grand getting it all started, and it took off.

Our first customer was from the USA. He was a gentleman that enquired about a hip and a knee replacement. He didn't have private medical insurance, so the treatment in America was going to cost him something like $80,000. He'd never travelled out of the USA, so we had to help him get a passport and arrange his flights and then he flew out to India for this treatment. When he went out there, one of the things they did was the pre-medical check because, obviously, this gentleman had never even had regular medical testing and they said, "Well, he's got a blocked artery and before we can operate on him, we're going to have to do heart bypass surgery on him." So, there we were just sitting in London, in our office, thinking, "What is going on here? We are completely out of our depth." But, actually, he had a fantastic experience; he got his heart bypass, recuperated, and then they did the knee and hip surgery and he went back to America.

I think we treated over 200 customers over that time and we got a lot of publicity. We were featured in *The Times* and on BBC news, as well as getting lots of radio interviews and various articles. It was great publicity but one of the things that we learnt is that, actually, turnover is vanity, profit is sanity, cash flow is king. We realised that what we were doing was developing a travel agency model and, actually, there really wasn't a business model there.

We'd got the entrepreneurial bug and we knew that we wanted our own business so we ended up considering other options. We were looking within the healthcare sector and we realised that there was this huge demand domestically. We had an ageing population and, as a result of that, we felt care homes would be a really good opportunity for us. Unfortunately, at that time, when we went to look at care homes and we spoke to the banks, they said, "One: you don't have experience. Two: you don't have enough money. And three: you're too young to buy a care home." That was quite disheartening for us but we persevered and, in the end, we realised that there was another option, which was looking after people in their own home: domiciliary care.

Mehul and I came across a franchise, Bluebird Care, and I think we were the first people to enquire with them, and we launched that back in February 2007. At that time, the whole purpose was delivering quality care for private, paying customers. The challenge was that the sector, at that moment, was 100% social services, so it was quite innovative but it was quite challenging because we were trying to set up a whole new marketplace. But, fortunately for us, we persevered. Many times, we came close to closing the business down and becoming bankrupt. But, when the recession happened, a lot of the care companies that were very turnover-focused collapsed and social services came to us and we were able to scale and grow that business very quickly. Last year was our ten-year anniversary and we've been rated outstanding by the Care Quality Commission (CQC), which puts us in the top 1% of care companies. Bluebird Care is now one of the largest providers of care at the home in the UK as well.

It was a very sharp learning curve because it's a very people-orientated business; it can't be systemised as much as other businesses might be. In 2008, Mehul came up to me and said, "We've got enough money in the bank account to last us for about three months." This was because we just weren't getting enough customers through the door. Then the recession happened and – I remember clearly – we had a phone call from three local councils on the same day, saying, "Can you take these customers on?" I think in our first year we turned over £100,000, then it went up to £500,000 in the second year and then we did £1.25 million in the third year and then it just scaled up at a very fast rate thereafter. We were completely out of our depth at that time because the business was just growing at such an electric pace. We were recruiting, we were taking on customers, and we were running around like headless chickens for the first couple of years. On the outside it looked great but inside we were working seven days a week trying to keep all the wheels spinning.

I think it hit a critical point. When we started our property journey, we came across a business coach and this was a very defining moment for us because he said, "Look, you've got a great business. You both have got great skill sets, which are very complementary, but what we now need to do is to help you run this business as if it is a £1.6 million business rather than a £100,000 business." That was a very significant moment for us.

An analogy of our journey would be a bit like playing Monopoly. We started very small, working on buying single-lets on Old Kent Road and Pall Mall, then developing the HMOs and the care business would have been like The Bow and Strand. Now, with the care homes, we're moving into the hotels. If you go for the hotels straight away, you're burning your cash and you could be out of a business unless somebody lands on you, and that's a matter of luck rather than business strategy. But if you start small and then build up your cash flow, and use that to invest in much better assets, over time, you'll start getting the hotels. I think Mehul's dream is one day to have a hotel on Park Lane or Mayfair but I think we've a long way to go yet. But it's about building that step-by-step strategy.

Going into the health sector when you're not medical sounds daunting.

Mehul: One of the things that helped us is that we made sure we recruited the people who did have the knowledge and experience. We had to find our own feet, and learn through experience. We got to know the health industry, the healthcare sector, by going to meetings with social services, health care forums, and so on. Also, by making sure we've got the care managers, the supervisors, and so on in place, because they're the ones who are dealing with the customers on a day-to-day basis. In the early days, we would go out and do the care work ourselves to really get a handle on what our business was about. We'd be there morning until night, either providing care or out dropping leaflets, trying to recruit carers. In the first couple of years, we were doing everything and anything just to build that business and I think that's what helped us really get a good 360-degree understanding of it. Then we put the right people in the right places. It was a massively steep learning curve but then, once we knew what the business was about, it was just about replicating it in the various areas where we provided care in Berkshire.

Tushar: I think the other thing, for Mehul and me, is that we wrote down what our values were. For the care business: quality, reliability, and being very professional, as well as having a passion. One of the things we've realised over the last ten years is that our core purpose is really about making a difference. I think when you're making a difference – whether it's in care or property development or even in your day-to-day life – you find that you are actually at your happiest. I think care gave us that opportunity to make a difference to people's lives. So, although we may not have had experience and knowledge, we were doing something we were passionate about. That gave us the energy to overcome the obstacles.

As entrepreneurs, we realised early on that you don't need to know everything as long as you know the fundamentals or you can recruit the right people who have that specific knowledge. I think one of the lightbulb moments is we're not looking at building businesses; we're about building teams that run our businesses. So, if we can recruit the right teams, with the right values, the right experience, and the right drive and passion, our businesses will grow and develop themselves. I think that's one of the things we look back on and think, "Wow. It's amazing." Our current area manager and our business development manager started off as a carer or a junior within our care business. Over the last eight to ten years, we've developed various roles into becoming leaders within our business. I think that's about us having a philosophy of building teams and then building businesses, and also about making a difference. Not just to our customers but also to our staff. I think when we've done that, and we focus on that, we know that it will work out regardless of the challenges and obstacles. If we don't have that philosophy, it becomes a real challenge and if we focus on the profit and the money, then it all falls apart. When we've done that in the past, it's been very challenging, because the profit and money will only come when you deliver a quality service to your customers and you look after your staff.

What led you to set up Centrum Group?

Tushar: We've got an eclectic, varying level of businesses, so we started off Bluebird Care and then we started off the property business. We were told that if we were going to be holding our properties long term as an investment, taking our money out of our care business as income, we were going to be taxed at 40% to 50%. However, if we created a group structure, we could transfer profits between companies quite freely. So, at that stage, we were advised to set up a group structure and that's one of the reasons why we set up Centrum Group.

Centrum Group is a holding company and within that we have our care business, our buy-to-let portfolio, our development company (which is Blenheim & Chester Developments), and we now have our new business, which is Centrum Care Homes, for which we recently acquired two large care homes. So, effectively, Centrum Group is our holding company and we have these businesses that sit underneath it. It's about making a difference, delivering a quality service, and building long-term cash flow and assets for us and the company.

How is your business different from other similar businesses?

Tushar: I think the most significant thing is we're a value-based business. Mehul and I have a really clear set of values and principles that we run our business on. Quality is one of those things; we won't do anything that isn't quality. When we looked at property, all our HMOs, all our properties, are done to a very high standard so it would be somewhere we would be happy to live or our children would be happy to live. When we look at the care business, the question we ask all our staff is, "Would you want your mum and dad to be treated this way?" And if the answer is no, then don't do it; if it's yes, then do it. Quality is very important to us. Integrity is very important to us. Passion is very important to us. Adventure and fun are important to us. There's no point doing something unless we're having fun and growing and developing ourselves. Also, building teams is important and continual development is an important element.

In our business, we have a very strong culture which is based on our values. I think everyone will say (even our staff and our customers) that we come as a team. If you took one of us out of our business, the business would be impacted. We have complementary skills that really become assets to the business. That then permeates into our staff so even within our care business operations, our operations manager, care manager, and business development manager are probably replicas of Mehul and myself. I think we're creating that culture and we're creating an environment where people feel that difference and I think getting an 'outstanding' rating from the CQC has been a reflection of that.

Also, the fact that our HMOs are always rented out; we don't have the void periods that some people may suffer from. Our tenants are happy to recommend us and help us with our properties. We know that we're doing the right thing; it doesn't feel stressful. When I speak to other landlords or other people running care businesses, they find it very stressful. We find that, actually, we have positive stress rather than negative stress.

What have been your challenges and learnings along the journey?

Tushar: One of the defining moments for us was around 2012. We were at a Tony Robbins' business mastery event and he put this model up and what he called it was 'The Entrepreneur's Journey'. When you start a business, you have a lot of enthusiasm; it's like a new-born child. You're loving, you're putting your heart and soul into it, and it doesn't matter if you're not making money because it's your new-born child. You'll do anything for that child. Then things start taking on a bit of momentum and you start to get a little stressed as you're out of your depth. You get to that early toddler stage where you think, "Oh, wow. Actually, this business is taking off." You're getting your first customers, your first staff, and it's still exciting; it's still all fun but hard work as things are constantly changing. Then you get to the more challenging stage, which is the teenage years, and this is where your business is really growing rapidly. But, like a teenager, you lack direction, you lack identity, you lack focus, you're moody and temperamental, and you think the whole world is against you. A lot of businesses at this stage fail because they've got so many things going on that they lack the focus and they lack that direction. Also, as a teenager, you're growing – the biggest thing for a growing company is cash flow. And, like most teenagers, you don't have the cash to fulfil all your needs. They want to do everything but they don't have the cash to do everything. So you need to get that focus and identity.

When he put that model up, I realised that's where we were in our business journey: that we were actually running out of cash because we were growing our care business, we were growing our property business but we were lacking a bit of focus and identity. Also, when things went wrong, we blamed the whole world rather than taking responsibility for it. It felt like us against the world. But, as a young adult, which is the next phase, you get a bit of focus and you start taking responsibility for your life and your decisions and you get a little more mature about things. But you also have the energy and the drive to make things happen. I think we managed to transition to that quite successfully. Because if you don't do that during your teenage stage, your business fails because you just have that lack of direction for growth. So, that's where we got to with the care business. We put the management team in place. Mehul was very good at putting the systems and the structure in place. I was good at finding the opportunities for growth and we worked in key areas.

It was the same with our property journey. When we started off, we were looking at everything. We were looking at lease options, local housing, repossessions, auction properties, student properties, HMOs, blocks of flats. We had no real strategy. Back in 2011, Mehul was very good analytically and he said, "Look, if we buy a single-let, this is how much money we're going to make. If we buy an HMO, this is how much cash flow it is going to be." In 2011, HMOs were also very challenging to finance because it was a new area; they didn't have the backing of the banks. But Mehul and I realised that what we wanted to do was – concentrating on our core values and principles – quality. We thought if we could get high-end HMOs for young professionals in good locations, these would increase the cash flow really well. So, that's what we started focusing on in our journey.

That worked really well. Because they were hard to finance, we got some really good deals. We got some long-term exchanges. We had one property that was 100% vendor-financed for us. The vendor, literally, put the title in our name and said, "You pay me a mortgage of 6% a year and then when you can afford to re-finance it, let me know and pay me my money back." You might wonder why somebody would want to give us their property for free but he was an old, retiring landlord, his kids weren't interested in taking on the properties, he'd had a heart attack and just wanted to get rid of his property. We realised that property isn't about the bricks and mortar; it is about helping people to solve their problems. If we could do it in an ethical and mutually beneficial way, that would be great for us. After we bought that property, we spent a lot refurbishing it, which was a challenge. But we were fortunate in that we were able to refinance it out and pay the vendor back his original money although because of the problems we experienced with the refurbishment, it put us off investing in HMOs for a while. So, we took a pause but, with hindsight, that was the wrong thing to do because we should have just dusted ourselves down and learned from the mistakes on that HMO.

Then, I think we came across an opportunity to buy a repossessed care home, which effectively was six bedrooms with six en suites, with a double-storey extension, and we bought it for £186,000. Three months later, the bank valued it at £330,000. We got all our cash out and all it required was a lick of paint, no planning changes, and that property now rents out for £3,300 a month and gives us a cash flow of £1,800 net profit a month and we've none of our money left in. Once we did that one, we realised the mistakes we made with our first investment property. We learned from that and applied it to our future investments and since then we've gone on to build quite a substantial portfolio of HMOs. They're all high-yielding and cash-flowing really well.

What have your biggest 'aha' moments been along the way?

Mehul: One of the biggest lightbulb moments for me was about four years ago. We started going into property development more aggressively and we still had the care business. What we decided was for Tushar to focus on the property development and for me to focus on the care business. But, in fact, I'm really good on the structural operational side – putting systems and processes in place. And Tushar is very good at the growing, looking at the ideas, the marketing, and the innovation side of things. So, when we split ourselves up to focus on the two individual businesses, they both suffered in their different ways. The care business was great in terms of running well on its own but the growth aspect wasn't there. With the property business, it grew fantastically but the systems and structures weren't there. What we realised, actually, was that we needed to work together on those businesses and then put the resources in place to support their growth and development.

So, from then on, every time we've gone into business or looked at ventures, we've looked at it from both angles. Our different profiles work really well together. If you were to put us in a box, I would be on one side and he would be on the other and we'd make a perfect square. That was a real eye-opener for us and I think we've built our teams in the same way. For example, in our care business, we've got an operations manager who looks after the compliance and the daily running of the business and we've got a business development manager to help sustain the growth and ensure that we're looking at new ways to get customers. So, in every business that we're now creating, we're using that same formula. I think that that was probably one of the biggest 'aha' moments for us, really.

I think the other thing that we've learnt along the way is to always make sure you have a plan A, B, and C because you don't know what to expect sometimes in any business journey. I think you've got to be very thick-skinned because you'll have good times, which you're going to enjoy, but there'll be a lot of rough times, when you're thinking, "Why am I doing this?" You're pulling your hair out and thinking, "Was I better off in the corporate world?" But when you look at the bigger picture, you see that it's not about the short-term view; it's about where you're going in the long term. That's quite important.

Your business has won quite a few awards.

Mehul: The biggest award we got was the Dementia Carer of the Year Award in 2010. That was the first major award that we received and that spurred us on and inspired the rest of the team. It gave such a boost to the team to say, "Let's apply for more during the course of the year." So, out of the whole of the UK, we were recognised as being the best dementia care provider for home care. Then a couple of years ago, we were also finalists in various other sectors.

Tushar: We've been recognised in a number of awards in the care sector. Within the Bluebird Care franchise, we've won numerous regional awards and were National Franchisee finalists as well. We've also, within the property business, been highlighted for our work in terms of crowdfunding and in 2009, we were the face of Funding Circle as part of their online campaign. We've not gone for personal awards because that's never been something that's been important for us. However, we realised that awards are quite rewarding for our team and are recognition of the work and effort that they've put in.

Last year, the CQC had to rate all the services and we got 'outstanding', which was a fantastic achievement because it made us realise that we're one of the best care companies in the UK, putting us in the top 1%. It's taken ten years to get there; lots of hard work and building the right team and culture to get that. This is why a long-term vision coupled with values and hard work is important.

What are your proudest achievements over the years?

Tushar: That's a really good question: one of the main things is making a difference. The teams that we've built are making a difference in our businesses and for our customers. We've created a lifestyle that allows us to make a difference. But I think the other thing is that it has allowed us to make a difference with our families. We're able to spend quality time with our families and give them the experiences – adventures, holidays, and opportunities – that, maybe, Mehul and I didn't have as children. I think that's something that gives us a lot of personal satisfaction.

The other thing is our opportunity to give back. We do a lot of charity work; I'm on the board of a national charity, so I do a lot of regular work with that. We take part in a weekly youth club where we're mentoring and helping local youth in the Reading area. Both Mehul and I are supporting orphanages and schools in Africa and India, which is something that we're very passionate about.

Another value of ours is having fun. Every year, we will choose a personal challenge, which we will then do to raise money for charity. So, last year, we did a challenge in the Brecon Beacons to raise money for Action Medical Research, which is a charity that raises money for medical breakthroughs for children. We had to cycle about 50 miles across the Brecon Beacons, climb a mountain, and paddle a canoe. Every year, we choose something that challenges us personally but also allows us to raise money for a good cause. Historically, I've done the London and New York marathons and Mehul's done other cycling challenges as well. It's something that allows us to make a difference as well as hitting our values of having fun.

Mehul: Looking back, if someone had told us 10 years ago where we would be now, we would have bitten their hand off to have multiple businesses and the flexibility to work when we want or where we want.

We're not chained to our desks or on a 9-to-5 treadmill. We can run our business and still have the flexibility to help others as well as spending time with our family as we've both got young children. Many of our friends who are in the city are working really long hours and hardly ever see their kids.

It's also great when our parents say, "We're really proud of you and what you've done." When we were children, they were constantly on our backs, saying, "You need to do your homework. You need to do this or that." So, it's quite nice when they now say, "I'm so proud of what you guys have become."

What advice would you give to someone else wanting to achieve what you have?

Mehul: I think a big thing is to do something that you're passionate about. When you don't have the passion, it comes through in the work you do. We all have our dips. About five or six years ago, I had a dip where I kind of lost that passion and you could see it coming through. I had to wake myself up again and say, "Look, why am I doing this?" All of a sudden, when you have that passion, people see it and it energises everyone else around you. Positivity breeds positivity. So, that's huge in terms of making sure you always try to stay as positive as you can; and don't make decisions when you are in a negative state because those tend to be the wrong decisions more often than not. Whereas if you're in a positive mindset, you're going to, most likely, make the right decisions.

Tushar: I remember Tony Robbins saying, "Most people underestimate what they can achieve in ten years and overestimate what they can achieve in a year." If you look back at our journey, that first year we had lots of cash flow challenges and we thought it would have been easier for us to quit and go back to the corporate world. But, by having a ten-year vision, a ten-year goal plan, and constantly working towards that, holding each other accountable and pushing each other, we've got there.

Ten years ago, we went to visit the banks looking to buy our first care home. That never happened and we were told we were too young. We didn't have enough money or experience to do this. Yet, ten years on, we've bought our first two care homes and just two weeks ago, the bank came back with another care home, which is failing, and they'd like us to have a look at potentially taking and running it because it's going to go into administration. It's a bit of a fire sale. The vendors are also open to us doing that because they're tired and exhausted from running the care home. So, it's funny that ten years ago, we were being refused but ten years on, we are now important to the people who said we couldn't do it.

Mehul: The Tony Robbins event was the defining point for us because we changed a lot of the limiting beliefs. When Tushar and I went to the event, we really couldn't afford it, so we put it on our credit card having no idea how we were going to pay for it. But that really blew away a lot of our limiting beliefs and set our goals and vision for the following five to ten years. So, that would probably be the best £500 investment we made. It really changed our perspective and ensured that we knew everything was achievable as long as you have the drive for it. It was life-changing.

It made us realise that we had lots of limiting beliefs which we needed to break from to fully develop. Everyone comes out of that weekend highly charged, with high energy, wanting to transform their lives, and when you go back to people, maybe six months or even six weeks later, they're just back to their normal routine.

Tushar and I really benefitted from being able to hold each other accountable. It's about setting mini-goals on a daily, weekly, monthly, quarterly, and yearly basis that are helping you get to your macro-goals.

Tushar: It's that slight edge principle; it's about doing something every day that pushes you towards your goals. I think it's important that you keep in mind that you're going to have setbacks in your life. Learn from them; move forward. I'm a big fan of Tony Robbins but that doesn't mean it's for everybody.

You've got to find something that really resonates with your core principles and then set your mini-goals on a regular basis and start achieving them. Then the momentum builds up and that will get you through your challenges and get you to your macro-goals quicker.

Another important piece of advice is to run your own race. Be inspired by other people, learn from people, but it's your life. You make your decisions based on what *you* want, not just because somebody else is doing something that you think is cool. So, run your own race and I think that's really important because then you make sure you don't get into the rat-race – and that benefits no one.

PETER ARMISTEAD

"I run my business remotely from overseas in Canada. I bought a house there because of my love of skiing/mountains and ultra-running."

Job Title: Property Investor and Developer.

Personal Bio: Property developer, investor and entrepreneur specialising in property in South Manchester.

Business: Armistead Property.

Services:

Development of residential property, property management, freehold management, property rentals, and sales. We design and build award-winning boutique properties. We manage properties on behalf of other landlords as well as having an extensive portfolio ourselves. We own and deal in ground rents and manage blocks of apartments.

Contact:

T: 0161 850 5588

E: info@armisteadproperty.co.uk

Website:

www.armisteadproperty.co.uk

♦ ♦ ♦

I run my business remotely from overseas, in Canada. I left my job as a lawyer in London in 2001 and bought a house in Canada because of my love of skiing, mountains, and ultra-running. I am a competitive ultra-runner and have competed in several world-class races. I have won races and am a regular on the podium at the 100-mile and 50-mile levels.

Running a successful business remotely has its challenges but with the technology available today it is a very doable proposition. You obviously need good staff on the ground for you, though.

What made you decide to leave your nice, safe job as a lawyer in London to become a property investor based in Canada?

I decided I wanted to be a lawyer some time before university. I did a degree at Durham University and then I went to law college in York for a couple of years. I trained at one of the big City firms and then moved in-house into an investment bank and worked there as a lawyer for four years.

I loved the law; it was exhilarating. I loved working in a big company as well. I like finance but the whole lifestyle element of it didn't appeal to me that much.

I was getting the best out of the London nightlife scene in my mid-20s; that was great. But I had an urge to set up my own business and live in the mountains.

So, in November 2001, after handing in my notice, I moved to Whistler, Canada and taught myself to be a property investor. That was 17 years ago.

What was your defining moment?

I first set foot on skis when I was 20 and that was a life-changing moment for me. I started searching out a ski resort I would like to live in while I was a lawyer. I literally went to Whistler for a one-week holiday with one of my friends in 2001. I was blown away by the quality of life over there: British Columbia was a province for me that just ticked every single box. It is one of the best places in the world to be outdoors and it's pretty much like a playground for adventurous adults. It was like I was on steroids. I didn't even know I wanted it until I went there. I went back to the UK, landed on Sunday, and resigned on Monday morning.

It sounds impulsive and simple but it was a pretty stressful process to go through. I was doing well as a lawyer: I had partnership (the goal of every lawyer) there on a plate within a year or two but the whole time I was a lawyer, I was unsatisfied. I wasn't happy being an employee sitting behind a desk the whole time. I looked at my boss and people ahead of me that I should have aspired to be like. Lovely people. Great people, most of them. But the end goal just wasn't satisfying or challenging enough. It was, basically, just staying on the treadmill for an extra few years and I knew I would get there, which just wasn't enough for me. So, I decided I was going to leave the law totally; I wasn't going to be a lawyer in a different country. I didn't want a sedentary job. I was going to set up my own business, move abroad, live in a ski resort, and run the business from there.

Initially, I had two businesses in tandem while I was a lawyer. I set up an online casino where people used to bet with me; I was the bookie, basically. That was in the early days, before regulation, back in the late 90s. I was actually one of the first people in the UK to get that going. It was alright but it never made the type of money that I wanted it to. The industry back then was in its early stages and there were a lot of challenges associated with that.

The other thing I was doing at the same time was real estate. Around 1997, just after I had qualified to be a lawyer, I bought my first house. It was a one-bedroom flat in Islington; I did it up a little, lived in it for a couple of years, then re-mortgaged it and moved out into a place in Brixton. Then I did the same thing there – lived in that place for a year or so, renovated it a little, new kitchen, etc – just amateur stuff. Then I moved out and bought a place in Clapham and did the same thing again. I then went on holiday to Whistler.

What gave you the confidence to hand in your notice and invest full time in property? Not many people would have the courage to do that.

I did have a bit of bravado and front back then. I was young and passionate. I still am. When I worked it out in my mind, everything was good: I was going to leave my well-paying job as a 'high-flying' city lawyer, live in the place of my dreams, set up a super-profitable business, and everything would be amazing. But every time I went to sleep for about six months, that's when the demons would come out in the dark. Deep down, I really didn't have that much self-confidence. I was leaving a job that I'd been training for for many years. I started the quest to be a lawyer before university and then three years at university, a couple of years at law college, a couple more years of articles, three or four years of working – and there I was, leaving it, just when the big money was coming in. It was quite a difficult time, really. But it was an overriding urge and I had to do it. My aim was to become a good skier – a really good skier. Skiing is a physical sport, so I needed to be in as good a shape as I could be and so I wanted to do it by the time I was 30, not after the years had ticked on and I was 60 and retiring. I wanted to turn the whole idea of working hard all your life then retiring to do what you really want to on its head. I wanted to make the big important 'what do you want to do with your life?' choices first and then make the work fit round them. It was hard to do. As for the confidence, it was a 'fake it until you make it' type of approach. There was a lot of soul-searching during that period.

What were your first steps to going full time in property?

Well, I realised a bunch of money while I was still a lawyer and still had the salary coming in, so I remortgaged my three London properties. It was not a lot of money by today's standards but it was enough that I could buy a place in Canada and have a bit left over for lifestyle expenses, living costs, and a small fund for some other property investment, wherever that might be. The whole time I was a lawyer, I was reading books about real estate, business, sales techniques, and negotiation techniques. Within a couple of years of leaving the law, I must have read over 100 books on setting up your own business and all the various skills that I needed. The more that I read, the more I was learning about property. It was real estate that I thought would be the way forward, and that's what I focused on.

What were your main challenges in the early years of your business?

The main things were setting up from scratch with no formal training in real estate and not much money. Back in the day, I didn't have much money, though in the early 2000s (around 2001 to 2007) you didn't necessarily need a lot of money. The market was very different to how it is today and you could do creative deals very easily with no money down. It was mainly a case of finding the deals and it was a good active market. The first six years were very easy in the sense that investment and trading conditions were good. The only challenge was to work as hard as I could and do as many deals as I could. I bought and sold well over 100 properties during this period.

I focused on one geographic area (South Manchester) and, quite early on, I met some great and inspirational people who are still friends and business contacts to this day. They were people who had solid business plans, which I was able to assess, copy, and improve on. It's as simple as that. I became friends with them, went out for coffee and beers with them, and they showed me what they were doing. I started emulating their business plan, then eventually changed it quite dramatically by focusing a lot more on the high end. My business plan for the first few years was a relatively low-end business but it enabled me to make good money by buying a lot of standard properties as quickly as I could.

What led to you choosing Manchester as the area to invest in?

When I was living in Whistler in early 2002, I went to a property course in Vancouver. After that, I created a business plan to have three very different property areas to invest in. So, I already had a few places in London: great. I had a couple of places by now in Whistler – a foreign country and a resort town very different to London with different factors affecting prices going up, prices going down, and rents. Then, the other area of real estate that I decided to choose was smaller, cheaper properties in the north of England.

For a year or so, I went to quite a lot of places doing my due diligence – Liverpool, Leeds, Manchester (where I'm originally from), Glasgow, Paisley. I met up with local investors and estate agents and checked them all out. I ended up picking Chorlton and Whalley Range in South Manchester as my preferred investment area.

I got a few places there and then I realised that one particular business plan worked better than the others.

Over the next few years, I got more and more places in Manchester and around 2005, I decided to put all of my eggs in one basket and focus mainly on South Manchester.

The reason for that was:

A) I had a very good business plan there; and

B) economies of scale.

I wanted to go from being an investor to running a proper business. By that, I mean I didn't want to outsource everything; I wanted my own property manager, who worked for me and would manage and rent out our properties, and I wanted my own maintenance guy or a team of them.

Investors generally get hammered by overheads: it takes 20% to 30% of your profit margin away instantly. I thought I'd set up a small business in Manchester, which I did, where I could control as many of the costs as possible. At this point, we had maybe 20 or 30 properties in Manchester so I hired a property manager who just managed my properties for me and it was cheaper than a lettings agent.

Now, I've got a couple of property managers and over 100 properties. We are the lettings agent now and we also rent properties out for other investors. I've got a couple of maintenance guys and they go around and look after all our properties. So, it was about creating a business rather than seeing property just as an investment.

What does your business do today?

We've got two distinct sides to the business. The main side is the development business. We've got about 20 builders, who we employ full-time, and we buy large unloved buildings that are about 3000 to 16000 square feet. They tend to be the old, run-down HMOs – properties at the end of their life. We buy them, regenerate them, make them look great and beautiful again, and then split them internally into apartments as high-end as the market will take. We tend to sell most of what we do but we also keep a good chunk as well.

Our rental properties are the second side of the business. We have an office with a couple of staff that manage the rental properties and a couple of maintenance people that look after them.

I manage my business and supervise the various aspects of it. The lettings staff on the rental side do most of the day-to-day work and I focus on the development side of the business. We employ property finders, architects, interior designers, planning consultants, builders, etc in our business and each one needs to be managed but left to do their job without micro-managing. All of our main staff are experts in their individual fields.

What is your company culture like?

As a medium-sized business, with around 25-30 workers, we look at ourselves as one big family, working together. We almost never have anyone leave us. The two head builders, who are brothers from Poland, have both been with me for 16 years now. I also employ their father, their younger brother, and the younger brother's wife and I've also employed their sister in the past, as well as many of their relatives. A few years ago, they decided that they wanted to move back to Poland, so we came to an agreement that they would keep a house in England (in Manchester) and commute backwards and forwards to work. They work two weeks for Armistead Property then they go home for two weeks. We've got two brothers doing that, so there's always one head builder on site and now, with their younger brother, there's another builder on site the whole time as well. We're very flexible.

Our architect lives in Spain. So, this morning, for example, I've had an hour-long Skype with my architect. I'm in Canada; it's pitch black over here. It was, literally, four in the morning Canadian time. He's in Madrid where it was getting on towards the end of the working day and we were both 100% focused on discussing real estate in

Chorlton. We're putting a planning application in for a block of 20 flats, which we bought in December, and that works well. We could have been sitting in Chorlton or we could have been sitting in our various places where we've chosen to live.

It's probably because I live in Canada that things have to be flexible, so I put a great emphasis on having a good team. You do anything you can to make it work. I've loaned workers money to buy houses in the past. I've bought them cars. Whatever they need to do their job efficiently and effectively, then we provide that. The average person that works for us has far more holiday than they would in any other average English company. My workers tend to be Polish, and have families in Poland, even though England is where they and their immediate families live. They like to go back to Poland for three weeks over Christmas, for two or three weeks over Easter, etc, so we make it work. It's a pretty casual, friendly atmosphere. We hook up after work and go for a bit of food and things like that. I like working in my company and I set a flexible culture.

Why do people choose you over your competitors?

One of the areas we focus on far more than most investors/developers is architecture and good interior design. We spend a lot of time at the front end of a development making sure we are maximising the potential of a building. Good design is time-consuming but the return on investment is good and your clients will pay a premium for a special property. It's also one of the most satisfying parts of the job: transforming old, unloved buildings into the best buildings in an area. By our good design, we have successfully raised the ceiling prices of apartments in both of our chosen postcodes in South Manchester.

Planning is a specialised area with a lot of law attached to it so you can't just dip in and expect to buy a plot of land and get planning permission on it. It's a complicated, tricky area. But, if you can get a plot of land, get the right planning on it, and then do a development, the biggest amount of money you will make is almost certainly in the planning uplift. Just by getting planning permission on a plot of land, it can change a plot of land that's worth £100,000 into a plot of land that's worth £1 million, easily. This is just by going through the planning application and instructing an architect. So, for us, that's absolutely key. We almost never do developments where we can't get a decent element of planning gain in them – whether that be sticking an extra couple of units in a basement or building an extension and putting five extra units in there or getting planning permission for a series of ten town houses on a plot of land, for example. These are all things that we've done. We focus a lot on planning law. I've got an amazing architect and also a really good planning consultant that works with us.

Once we've got planning permission, then the architectural and design side carries on being amazingly important. We specialise in renovations; we don't do new builds. We want old properties that are rundown and unloved. We want to be able to recycle them and get them back to their former glory, looking as timeless as possible from the outside. I don't mean trying to copy exactly what was there back in the day because some of those small windows and other features are just not appropriate today. But we will do as good a job as we can to restore them and make them look stunning. If we need to put an extension at the back where we've got big windows to let more sunlight in, we will do that. But we really want to do an amazing architectural number on them externally and internally, when you walk through the front door.

How has it worked for you being a big fish in a small pond?

Our business plan is to be the best in our area. We only focus on a few postcodes in South Manchester and we currently only do renovations of less than 30 units, ideally in buildings that have some architectural attraction. This enables us to really know our area and our market. We have good or preferential agreements with local suppliers and great relationships with the local agents.

You are always on show when you do a job. It's got to be great work as our reputation is on the line in a way that it isn't if you just do a one-off job. The unintended upside is that now, after doing 400 to 500 renovations locally over the last 17 years, we can see whole patches of our area which have been transformed from old, ugly buildings to some of the best in the area.

When I set out, I had no property in Manchester, or specifically the M21 or M16 postcodes. I met people that did – people that were probably very big fish in those postcodes and in Didsbury, especially. Business was quite easy for those guys. They picked up their phone and it was an estate agent on the end telling them about a deal that hadn't quite made it to the estate agent's window yet but perhaps they'd want to have a look at it. They got first refusal on deals as they had good contacts so I set out to try to do that too. You can't do it overnight; you need to build a reputation. You need to show that your work's good. You need to prove that you can do deals. If we agree to do a deal, we make sure that the deal is one that we want to do and then we do it. So many people agree deals, shake a hand on it, then back out and it never goes through to exchange. They've wasted everyone's time: the estate agent's, the lawyer's, everyone's. Whereas we know what we're doing because we've been doing business in the same area for 17 years.

So now, I am the guy that gets the phone calls. I pick up my phone, and I answer my emails rather than having to walk around the estate agents every Saturday morning saying, "Have you got any deals?" The estate agents give me deals and they know what I'm looking for, so they don't waste my time. I make sure that they're very well looked after in return. I'll buy the deal and they'll get their fee. When I sell the deal, they sell the properties for me. So, being a big fish in a small pond is absolutely key to my business plan.

How do you balance living in Canada with having a business in the UK?

I guess it is unusual. Before the Internet, you couldn't really do that. It would have been inefficient. Now, I have all the resources that I need on the Internet and telephone so I can run the business very well while I'm over in Canada. I do make compromises. I would make more money if I lived all year in the UK. As it is, I commute to work. I live three weeks in Canada, then do one week in the UK. That tends to be my main pattern. The downside is that there's a lot of travelling involved but it does enable me to run a successful business and we are the best developers in our area, so it clearly works. The key is having a business that is very well systematised and has good reporting mechanisms (as well as the best workers!).

What are the lightbulb moments you've had over the years?

I've had many 'aha' moments. One of them was sitting down and talking with one of my early mentors, maybe in 2001/2002, and I saw his business plan. It was buying large houses that were either already flats or getting planning permission on them to split them into flats. It was a really good business plan. It's been done in London for many years. Not as many people in Manchester were doing it yet. The buildings in Manchester are really nice; we have some really big sexy buildings out there. I looked at his business plan and thought that the blocks of flats idea was really good. Being able to own a whole block rather than an individual flat gives you so many more options. The actual freehold of the property has intrinsic value itself. So, that was one 'aha' moment. That's what I started doing.

Then I very quickly realised that there was definitely a market for the higher-end stuff. As a lawyer in London, I was used to good, comfortable types of apartments. The stuff in Manchester all seemed to be lower-end and damp. The private rented sector in Manchester was, 20 years ago, pretty low-quality in my area. I saw lots of low-end/slum landlords renting out horrible flats in old knackered buildings for low rents. The buildings were actually amazing, it's just that they were unloved and neglected. In London, those buildings would have high-end apartments inside and would sell or rent for a premium. Almost no one was doing this in Manchester back then, so I thought, "Okay, we can up that. I'm sure there is a market for it there." I started buying up these old, unloved properties and transforming them into the best properties in the area. I did it small-scale at first, established that I was right and that there was a demand, and then increased my business plan.

Over the years, we changed our business plan to create higher-end properties. My wife is an award-winning interior designer from Vancouver. She's used to doing big blocks of 400 apartments. When we married, she got involved in the business. She was absolutely key in giving us a good kick. Instead of it just being blokes making bloke decisions without any type of interior or architectural training between us, she gave us the design element, so from 2006 onwards we started designing nice, smart apartments, slowly but surely. We got ourselves a good award-winning architect on board as well. Just recently, the culmination of all this is that we won the UK Property Awards 2017 and for our last two projects we did amazing work and successfully raised the ceiling prices both in Chorlton and then in Old Trafford for apartments. So, there obviously is a demand for high-level apartments in good renovated properties.

What were your biggest challenges as your business grew?

There are loads of little challenges every single day. Some are great problems to have; others are not. There's been one very big problem that we've had to deal with and that was the crash of 2008. We had a tough time staying afloat and carrying on doing business during that period, although I am proud to say that we didn't sack anybody during this period. We had to look after all of the guys and girls that were working for us. That was ridiculously hard to do and there were many, many sleepless nights for a couple of years there.

Like most developers, at the time we were doing business with the Royal Bank of Scotland. The RBS was the biggest landowner in the country. Back then, they'd lend money to anyone that wanted it, pretty much. So, by 2007, we had a good few million outstanding with the RBS. Then they went bump in 2008. After being bailed out by the government, they started a very aggressive process of going around as many of businesses as they could, finding which were the semi-decent ones and really putting the thumb screws on. The irony is that they were looking at the good businesses, ones which made money, not the bad ones. So, any business that was good, and they could see money coming in and out and there were some good assets, those were the businesses that they went after to try and get as much money as they possibly could.

I had lots of meetings with the RBS during this period, which tended to be stressful events. Basically, the gist was, "We want all of our money back." I wasn't able to do that right away, so we had to get a staged plan. We had about four or five blocks outstanding with them, which was several millions' worth of lending. We couldn't refinance and no-one was lending money in 2008/9. So, we made a three- or four-year plan whereby I would pay them a lot more interest than I wanted during this period.

I had to do up the properties slowly but surely out of my own money, sell them on, and get them all off the RBS's books. So, we basically worked for the RBS for three or four years. It was like swimming under water but we managed to do it. The business was probably at the same level that it was at three years before but we'd emerged from it clean, clear, and without the banks on our back.

Did you ever feel like giving up?

For my leisure time, as well as skiing, I run races in excess of 100 miles; I'm an ultra-runner. I have run for 33 hours solidly, with almost no rest during that period, so I'm used to long, hard slogs. I wouldn't say I necessarily enjoy it but it's something that I'm conditioned to and used to doing. That was part of it, I think. After the good times, the bad times come. It's always like that. Even the Bible talked about seven years of good and seven years of bad. It's been going on forever. You're never going to stop cycles. No government, no Bank of England can do that; it's going to happen. It's just that that was a particularly rough and nasty time. I love a challenge and even when things were unpleasant and not fun, the challenge made me get through it. There's no way I could ever give up.

What are your top tips for mistakes to avoid?

Avoid building where you don't really have a good grasp of your client base. If you're producing anything, you need to know who's buying it and understand what they want. A lot of people go into it and they build something that's not appropriate or that's just below average. The average standard of building in England is pretty bland. You can do a lot better than that.

Avoid starting a deal or a construction build without having all the money ready. I see people getting into a mess with that all the time. They are so keen to do a deal that they jump right in. They can maybe buy the property but they can't afford to do anything to it. Or, they can afford to do half the work and they think that they'll find the money somewhere else. Or, I see quite a lot of developers using unrealistic figures – they just want to do a deal, so they make the figures fit. It doesn't work. You've got to be on top of your figures and not start a deal until you've got all the money ready to go.

Also, avoid letting someone else do your work for you without verifying what they say or do.

What are your top tips for newbies to property?

Work hard. Make yourself the world expert in what you do. Always manage people who are working for you: lettings agents, lawyers, architects, estate agents, accountants, property sourcers, builders, etc. Make sure you have systems in place and keep in constant communication. I got gazumped in one of my first deals, for example, and it was because my lawyer was being too slow and I let him.

Newbies to property need to network as much as they can. Find good people: if you've found a good person, they're worth their weight in gold. Don't do business with people that you don't really like. You can do a one-off transaction with someone you don't like, buy a property from them, that's fine. But if it's a day-to-day relationship – an agent, a property sourcer, and so on – make sure you have a good relationship with them.

Know who's going to be giving you money at the end of the day. If you're a developer, know who's buying your properties. If you're an investor, know who's renting your properties. Give them what they want.

Control the cash flow but don't be tight. Sometimes you need to spend money in a big picture type of way. Sometimes, you can't work out if it's going to give you a payback or not.

Make little strategic investments every now and again: if they work, then you can roll them out on a bigger scale. For example, we used to sell flats without dressings in them. My wife thought it would make a big difference if we dressed a flat but I was unsure. She made me do it anyway. She dressed one flat in a block of six – and the dressings ended up selling all of the flats.

So now, in every block, we have a show flat and it's a very good return on investment.

What are you proudest of?

There's a few things. Transforming many old distressed buildings into the best buildings in the area. Providing full-time jobs to 20-plus people, and many more by way of the money we spend and the services we provide locally.

Our biggest success to date is becoming the best developer in our chosen area of South Manchester and also winning the UK Property Awards Renovation Prize 2017 for Carlton Terrace, a boutique development of 16 apartments.

I'm proud of making it through the 2008 recession and managing to assemble a truly fantastic team. There's one amateur in my business: that's me. Everyone else is outstanding at their job. As I mentioned earlier, my wife's an award-winning interior designer. My architect is an award-winning architect. My builders are award-winning builders now and are producing the best flats in the area. If I walk around my two postcodes, I know the people that I do business with; it's a really nice environment. Of course, there are always problems but I work with some truly excellent people: people that I like as friends as well as business contacts. I get on with most of the local agents very well. So, I think I'm in a very privileged position now.

I come across a lot of people in business who are always moaning and complaining about people that either work for them or they're doing business with and the next thing you know, a deal goes wrong, or there's always a big problem lurking about for them. I'm really lucky. Everyone that I do business with on a day-to-day basis, I really like and they're really good at their jobs. If you're doing business with people like that, it seems to be easy. We always end up doing deals and having fun at the end of the day. So, I'm really proud that I've got such an amazing team working for me.

SULEMAN NAUKHEZ

"They feel like somebody actually cares, and they're not just a number... You can make a really big difference to their lives."

Job Title: Director.

Personal Bio: Specialising in sales, lettings, and management services. Property investor and entrepreneur.

Business: Property Link International Ltd.

Services: Residential and commercial sales, lettings, and management. Service provider to local authorities. Serviced apartments.

Contact:

E: info@propertylinklondon.com

T: 020 8554 8554

Website:

www.propertylinkuk.com

◆ ◆ ◆

T he first memory I have of property was when I was around five years old, when my dad was setting up the business. I remember helping him decorating the office and holding down the wallpaper for him while he was gluing it and sticking it onto the walls.

My dad came here in the mid-70s and he worked in finance. Initially, he worked in factories – I think a lot of people did at that time – and then he moved to London and went into banking. That's where he dealt with mortgages and insurance and he got into property from there.

The business started in 1989. We were living above the office at that time; we had a one-bedroom flat upstairs and a shop downstairs so my dad would be working there from morning till late in the evening. So, when we came home from school, he would still be in the office. Growing up, from day one I've been involved in the business and kind of helping everything along.

When we first started, it was very hard and financially, we weren't very well off. It was my father and his older brother: both families were living in that one-bedroom flat, though only for about two years because the market at that time was just picking up so, initially, we did very well and were able to move into a six-bedroom house. The families were living together because we were quite close. My father came to the UK first, his elder brother came shortly after and they lived together. Even when my dad went back and got married later on and my uncle did the same, they came back and still stayed together.

I grew up living with my cousins and uncle and auntie, so we had a very strong, big family, and that filtered into the business as well because it was mainly family members that were working in the offices. We had a few staff members after the first couple of years, but it was always a nice family environment. I never really saw it in the form of a hierarchy – this person working under this person – it was more like everybody working together. That's the environment I grew up with and learned from.

I had a few Christmas temp jobs when I was about 16 or 17, working in retail, part-time here and there. That was what all my friends were doing at that time, so I wanted to do that as well even though I'd been involved in the family business. Nearly every weekend my dad would get me to help out, probably because we couldn't afford the staff initially, but later on, it just became normal for me to become more and more involved. Even though I was so young, I would be with my dad when he went to his meetings or when he went to show properties or value properties. I remember him saying to me hundreds of times that he wanted to pass on his knowledge to me so that I wouldn't have to wait 40 or 50 years to learn what he had learned.

I remember going to meetings with him at the councils where I would be 11 or 12 years old. I would be sitting there with the head of housing or head of planning, and I would be taking notes. All those experiences got me wanting to be more involved in that business and wanting to be a part of it rather than going into anything else.

Later on, in university times, when I saw my friends going in other directions – getting jobs, doing graduate schemes, and so on – I used to think that maybe there were some other things that I should look into because I felt like I'd never really explored anything other than property, and I thought there might be other things that were better than this. But every time I looked into any other type of other business, I realised that the people at the top were investing in properties. So, that's what made me firmer in my decision to stick with properties and develop my career in that.

I was working in the office up to the age of about 16, doing basic admin work, going in on weekends and in the school holidays. I would be working in the office along with my younger brother as well, even my cousins.

After doing a few part-time jobs in retail, I decided to take on a proper role in the office and started going into the sales and letting side. My father wanted us to know all the ins and outs of the business; to know every role inside out. So, we've been in every role possible within our company and we know what each role involves and what needs to be done – so that now, when it comes to managing staff, we're in a much better position to do that.

Initially, I was doing sales: buying and selling over the summer holidays after my GCSEs. We're originally from Pakistan, and during this time a lot of our other family came here as well. After setting up the business and becoming financially stable, my father helped a lot of family to shift to London. By the time I finished my GCSEs, most of our family were here. Our parents decided that would be good for us if we went and studied in Pakistan for a few years, mainly because they didn't want us to lose our culture and also to get to know our relatives there. They wanted us to experience a different type of culture that you don't really get when you've been brought up here. In October 2011, we went to Pakistan and got admission into a private school which was affiliated with the Cambridge International Examination Board. I studied A levels there and then came back and went to university in London.

Those two years in Pakistan taught me a lot of things that completely changed my mindset and my attitude towards what I wanted to do and what I wanted to achieve. Over here, being in school and doing GCSEs, you don't really understand the value of what you're doing and the opportunities that you have. When we went to Pakistan and we saw what was there – even though we were in a private school and living in the capital city of Islamabad and living in a nice house – you still get to see the very poor living conditions. Even within the private school that we were going to, with very high fees, you still get people who are from very different backgrounds and who are not as wealthy as everyone else.

So, you mix with a lot of different types of people and that makes you realise the sacrifices that are made just to get a good level of education.

That really hit me when I came back here and went to university. People take so much for granted: the opportunities we have in London and being here where we have all these facilities. People leave their families, they leave their children behind, so that they can come and get that. That made me want to work even harder and appreciate the opportunities that I had.

When I came back, I had a disagreement with my father about going to university because my plan had been to join the family business.

I couldn't understand why he wanted me to go to university and spend three years there, instead of joining the family business straight away. Eventually, I had to listen to my father and I ended up going to university. I think this was a good experience. I was still working a lot in the family business while doing my degree, and I was probably putting 60% of my attention on the business and 40% on my degree.

Eventually, once I'd finished university, I realised that having the degree was an advantage. Even though, theoretically, I might have not learnt much to do with business, just the skills of speaking to people and doing presentations and speaking in front of people and building relationships helped a lot later on. When I finished university, I was at an age and a level where I could take over a lot of responsibilities from my father. I realised that a lot of the skills that I learnt in university came into play, and it did really help in moving forward.

My father was still running the business while I was at university, but any time I could get I would be in the office, working on how to grow the business, how to expand, how to go into different sections of the property industry, and exploring different areas. We went from just doing letting and management, then we started doing sales, we started doing short-term lets, we started doing serviced apartments, and then we started getting into construction and development as well.

We spread our wings quite wide. We started getting into a lot of different projects and then explored all the different ways that we could use our investments and expand the business and then, from doing maybe about five or six different projects in the space of about two years, we realised that we were spreading ourselves too thinly. Our main skillset over the years was that we'd been very localised and we'd been giving a very personal service to all our clients, but it was moving away from that and I don't think the clients liked it as much.

So, after dipping our toes into the different markets, we decided to stick with our core business, which we were doing with the councils. Our main business is where we're providing accommodation for the social housing needs of all the councils: housing for homeless people; temporary accommodation for people who are on the waiting list to get a permanent home. This includes houses, flats, HMO buildings. We've been involved in that since 2001: it was the first contract that we got. We were actually providing properties for the council even before that, but we officially got nominated as the main supplier in 2001. We've expanded on that and now we are working with around 15 local boroughs and authorities in London.

With that part of the business, it's about working very closely with the councils and the housing associations, which get targets from the central government about how they need to reduce homelessness within their local areas. We work with the council to look at the figures that they've been given and see how we can try to work within their budget and achieve those targets that they've been set.

Because we've been working with them for such a long time, we get to sit in these meetings with them, with the housing minister and the head of housing in different local authorities. Obviously, these people have a lot of experience and knowledge of their local areas, so our clients also benefit from all this expertise.

With that side of the business growing, it's also grown our sales side because we have a good feel for where the best areas for investments are and where the property values are going to be getting higher. We'll be able to pick out the hotspots and our investors will be able to benefit from that.

One of the key things with our own investments has been that, mainly because of our religion, we don't take loans and we don't take any interest payments. That was a bit of a hurdle for us in the beginning because any estate agent that does sales also does mortgages, and we've never done mortgages and we wouldn't even recommend any mortgage suppliers because of our religious obligations. When clients came to us, we would tell them to go to a mortgage broker to get their mortgage. We did it in that way and it still kind of worked for us.

I have seen how my father is very strict in his religious obligations and in the way he does his business dealings. It's made me realise that you don't always need to be a harsh salesperson or a stereotypical aggressive businessperson. You can be honest and straightforward, and you can be calm and friendly and still get the job done. I think that being very religious has given my father his principles and it has trickled down into the business, and that's become the business ethos as well.

This is one of the main selling points that our investors like about us: the type of service that we give. Even when we are training our staff, we're telling them that we're not looking for the sale to happen today. When clients come to us, obviously, we want the business, but properties are the biggest asset that most people have. Most of the time, it's their whole life savings that they've invested into a property and if anything happens to that investment, it's their whole life and their families that will get affected.

The way we see it is we need to give the right advice for them at that time when they come to us. A lot of times that might mean that we're not getting business from them straight away. We might have to advise them, "It's not the best time for you to sell right now; it might be better for you to wait a year or two." That may mean that we're not going to get that business on that day but, because we've told them that in an honest, ethical way, when it does come to a year or two down the line, that same person will come back to us and that's what we teach everyone that works with us. I think it's these types of things that have helped us to grow and become so well-respected within the local community.

When I'm in the office, for example, somebody will come to tell me that their father bought a property from my father and their grandfather was a tenant living in that property before that. So, we've got two or three generations of people that have come to us and the next generation is still coming back to us – and it's all been because of the positive dealings that they've had with us. It's been through word-of-mouth: our clients have a good experience and they've gone and told other people.

My dad always sees marketing as a waste of money; he's from that generation. I think he has it in his head that if you need to spend money to market yourself, it means your service is not good enough. People that are using your service should like it so much that they go out and tell other people. That's how good your service should be, and that should be your marketing.

I think that's another reason why we've concentrated on the local area that we've been dealing with – because every time we've tried to expand and gone into other areas, our service has slipped. Every time our service standards go down, we step back and look at it again. We pride ourselves on our service. We don't want to be doing anything that forces us to drop our level of service.

Our main ethos is that any person that comes to us should be receiving good value and advice from us. That means when they do need you for business later on, they'll come back to you rather than go to any of your competitors. All of this has been very good for us growing locally and being a name in the local community and earning respect; people know how we work and what our ethics are. But now I've reached a stage where I'm married, and I've got children and I want to grow the business, I've realised that it's hard for us to grow because we are so involved in the business and with every client that we work with. We're obviously limited in how many people we can deal with. To expand, we need to teach and reinforce these principles and ways of working with our staff.

Understanding where my dad's been successful and understanding how we need to grow the business, we need a balance of both so we can continue to expand the business in a way where we don't lose the level of service or the reputation that we've built up but, at the same time, we are able to expand to a bigger level so that we can help more people and be helpful to other areas and go into other communities.

What I'm concentrating on now, moving forward, is trying to learn and implement systems and processes that will allow our staff to work in a way that will still hold on to our ethics and ethos but, at the same time, will allow us to concentrate on the growth of the business rather than being the face at the forefront of the business.

Around the end of 2016, I took a year out, and I went to seek help from mentors who had been in the industry for longer than me or who had certain systems in their business that they had already implemented successfully.

I spent time with other people who had other estate agencies that had been covering many more areas and regions than ours, seeing how they operate and how they run their businesses. Then I did some leadership training courses as well, just to try and improve my skills in how I'm going to be managing the staff and increasing their skills.

My dad has officially retired now, so I've got full control of the business. Moving forward, we're implementing a lot of new things in the business – new software, a lot of automation, a lot of new processes – which is pretty hard because we work in such a unique way compared to other estate agents. We still want to be able to give that personal touch to the clients as that's our main selling point and we don't want to lose that. So, at the moment, I think that's my core focus for maybe the next six months or so. I'll be working very closely with the staff members in each department and I am implementing certain processes and procedures that will help us to grow further.

That all sounds very positive. Tell me about some of your obstacles and challenges along your journey.

One of the main obstacles was when I finished university. Because of me having that mindset of wanting to grow and expand, the first thing I did straight after my degree was to open up another branch of our company, another office, in 2010. It was just before the Olympics happened so we decided to open our office in Stratford, in the area where the Olympics was happening, so that we could benefit from that. In hindsight, I feel like I wasn't really ready for it, but at that time I was very enthusiastic, so I just jumped right in.

Initially, it started off very well. We were working very hard, putting in long hours and implementing everything that I had learned over the years, working in my dad's office. We were still working together, but it was just a completely different branch, in a completely different area, and I had full control of what was happening in that branch. I think in all the excitement of wanting to grow, I put too much on my plate and I had too much to do because I was involved in every department of the business. Even though we had an established brand, it wasn't known in that area, so it was a bit like establishing a new business and growing it at the same time. I was involved in the sales and lettings and management, and then the accounts and all the levels that come with running your own business...

The sales and marketing which I'd been studying I was very good at, but the accounts side I found harder. After a year of running that business, I had to step back in order to keep my sanity and spend time with my family. I had too much on my plate and I couldn't handle it, and I felt like I was just hitting a wall. It demotivated me a lot. That was probably the hardest time. I wanted to grow the office but I wanted to be able to spend more time with my family as well, so I was stuck in the middle and wasn't sure what to do. My dad was very supportive throughout that period.

Eventually, we reached an agreement. My dad realised, as well, that he'd spent his whole life running the business. I was always involved in the business, so he spent a lot of time with me. But with the rest of my brothers and sisters, who are all younger than me, it was harder for him. He would be at the office and when he would come home, they would probably be asleep; in the mornings, they would usually be at school by the time he left. He would hardly get to see them or spend any time with them.

I think that was the main thing that got him to agree to kind of let go and be happy with the idea of handing over responsibilities to other staff members. My dad's always been very religious, so he gives a lot of time to mosques and charities as well, helping them with fundraising or just helping with arranging the events, so he's taken more of a backseat and is getting more involved in those projects now.

As a business, we've always been involved with these charities, and we've had fundraising events where the whole company's been involved. Sometimes, we've participated in charitable events as a company where all the employees would go down and have a day where we help to raise money. Now, I think my dad feels like he should give back and concentrate more on that, so he's let me take over and control the business a bit more.

My father and I have always just had the attitude that if you want it done right, you do it yourself. But I think my ideas started to change and I began to realise that if you're going to do it yourself, you can only do a certain amount and then you don't have any more time. The way to get past that is to train other people and delegate responsibilities.

So, I took some time off to study leadership techniques and how to implement certain structures and processes. It was that transition in attitude about how to run the business which was the main struggle for both of us. My dad set up the business back in 1989 and he's always done it in a certain way – so for him to let go of that and let me run in it a slightly different way was quite a big step.

The main thing that held it together was that we both had the same goal: we both wanted freedom to be able to do things with the family. During the time when I was growing up with my brothers and sisters, we hardly ever had any outings or did things that the whole family would do together. No one would ever be available at the same time; everybody was busy doing their own thing. My father and I would be busy with the business most of the time.

We have two main offices now and we're in the process of restructuring and implementing new processes and systems in the business.

What would you say has been your biggest success or achievement that you're proudest of?

We do a lot with temporary accommodation with the councils. The type of people that we are helping are people that have all of a sudden lost their accommodation. They might have been in rent arrears with the council previously, or with a landlord, and they've just been evicted and they've got children and they've got, literally, nowhere to stay. These are the sort of people that we help. We will find them a place, something that will be close to where their children are going to school. If they've got religious obligations, we will find somewhere they can go to pray locally as well. And when we've done that for people, after a couple of months, when they've settled in, they've come back to us. This has happened many, many times because this is the daily business that we do. These people come back to us and tell us how the children have settled down or how from being completely on the street, they've stabilised their life now and they're working properly and they feel like that we've done so much to help them. From our side, all we've done is our daily job. That's what we do on a day-to-day basis, so we don't feel like we've gone out of the way. But for them, it's such a big thing and they feel so overwhelmed by the fact that somebody would help them. That feeling is what makes me just want to do more of the same. That's when you feel like, "Okay, I've done something that's been worthwhile," and it's that feeling that makes you want to do it again.

They feel like somebody actually cares and they're not just a number. Especially when they come into your office, and they've got the children with them – they come in with a couple of suitcases, and pushchairs with children,

and that's all they have, and they've got nowhere to go –
when you've helped someone in that situation, that feels
good. We can normally help them to find temporary
accommodation within a day, or a couple of days at most.
It wouldn't be longer than that because these are people
who are in major situations where they've literally been
made homeless, so they need something urgently. These
people, because they're homeless, don't really have a
choice, and any property would do for them. But it's not
about giving them any property. You have to put yourself
in their situation: where they've got children, they've got
work, and they've got certain responsibilities and, alright,
they're homeless, but you don't want to make their life so
hard that you give them a property where they have to
travel far to take the children to school or to get to work. If
you actually try and listen to their problems and help them
according to what their needs are, they really appreciate it
and you can make a really big difference to their lives.

They can be in quite a distressed state when they come
to us, because they've been sitting in the council offices
for hours in the waiting areas for someone to see them,
and they've sometimes spent a couple of days trying to
just get the front of the queue and get allocated
somewhere. Sometimes, you might have to temporarily
put them somewhere and then within a few days, you shift
them to somewhere a bit more convenient. These people
don't have money in the first place and then, on top of
that, when they're shifting houses and having to move

around a lot, it's a lot more expensive for them. Even with the council, they don't really get subsidised much. Obviously, at the end of the day, we're a business as well, we're not a charity, but we try and help them as much as we can. They do seem to appreciate that we are genuinely trying to help them and we're listening to their problems.

What advice would you give to anyone else who wants to do something similar to you?

Whenever I speak to anyone and tell them that I'm an estate agent, they get *that* look in their eyes. Everyone thinks estate agents are very harsh and in-your-face salespeople; stereotypically, that's how they're perceived. Seeing how my dad works has made me believe that it can be done in another way. When you are taught sales and marketing techniques, you're never really taught to be genuine. But I've seen situations where even if my dad's made a mistake, or you know something's gone wrong in a deal, he would still be honest with the person, explain to them what's happened, and they would really appreciate that.

Whenever I'm negotiating a deal with someone, or I'm giving advice, I will always tell them what I would do if I was in their position and give them the exact same advice. It's easy to do because you're being genuine; you don't need to think up any schemes or anything like that. You're just telling them from your experience what is the best thing to do. I think when you are being genuine like that, the person you're talking to can actually tell that it's not a sales pitch, it's actually honest advice that's coming out.

It's about integrity: I think that's the main thing in any business. If you're on a low level, you can maybe win business over just because of your sales pitch. But when you get to a high level, and you are dealing with pretty experienced businesspeople, they can very quickly work out if you are the type of person with principles or just someone who is throwing out sales pitches. Just having that genuine character is what makes you successful in business, as people understand that if they do any sort of business with you, they are going to have honest dealings.

It's about having core values and principles in the business. This was covered while I was studying leadership techniques and how to motivate people: as a leader, you need to lead by example and show others how it's done. If you show your staff a way to do it through sales pitches and sales techniques, to me, that seems like you are deceiving your clients rather than genuinely adding value to them. It's much better to give good advice that will be useful to them. That is what is going to keep clients coming back to you. That's the main thing we try and teach our staff.

MIKE FRISBY

"A lot of the famous entrepreneurs are dyslexic. It's just the way that their brain is wired; I think that helps them do what they do."

Job Title: Property Investor and Developer.

Personal Bio: With over a decade of experience, I currently work on property investment deals between £300K and £3m. If you are stuck with a deal, or want a better return on your funds and want to get involved in property, please get in touch. In the past, my investors have gained returns in excess of 25% pa. I'm also host of Regent's Park Property Investors' Networking Meeting.

Business: Brankin Developments Ltd.

Services: High-end HMOs. Mentoring. Property development.

Contact:

T: +44 1483 516 299

E: pa@mikefrisby.co.uk

Websites:

www.mikefrisby.co.uk

www.brankinproperties.com

◆ ◆ ◆

I had my strengths and weaknesses in the classroom. Some of the school days were good; some of the school days were not so good. I was far more biased towards maths and science subjects and would be at the top for those. But when it came to English and languages, I was nearer the bottom, which used to frustrate me.

I don't think my dyslexia was ever formally diagnosed. It's only because I now have children with dyslexia that I realise that I had it. Often, with dyslexia, you know a lot but you struggle to get what's in your head down on a piece of paper. I have a lot of the traits of dyslexia: I know I keep a lot in my head. All three of my children have dyslexia to different degrees: some quite badly, some less so. I didn't have it severely, but I'm sure I have it.

It was in the days before dyslexia was commonly known. I do think it's given me a little bit of the drive that I've got today. You often see a lot of dyslexics end up as entrepreneurs because they don't always fit into big organisations. I see it as a good thing because I think differently; I problem solve. I'm used to having to work harder than most to make things happen, so for me it's a good thing. I see the struggle in my children as well; I see the frustrations with them and I think they have to work extra hard to get to the same place as many other people. I think that will stand them in good stead later in life.

Who were your early role models?

My parents were my early role models. My dad used to run a business, so from a young age that's what I thought I would do. I looked around and thought, "The people who have money seem to be people who own their own businesses." Although I went into the corporate world after I left university, I always thought I would run my own business eventually. I just needed to work out what that business would be. So, I would say my father was my role model and then some of the obvious entrepreneurs such as Richard Branson, who is also dyslexic. If you look at a lot of famous entrepreneurs, often you find that they are dyslexic. It's just the way that their brain is wired; I think that helps them do what they do.

As a child, when I looked at my dad running his own business, I could see it was hard work, but I could see that it also gave him good rewards. I thought it was pretty cool. He ran one business and then sold it. Then, he ran a couple of others and did various things with the proceeds of selling the first. I had a nice upbringing and I saw a good life coming from it, so that reinforced my view. I knew deep down that I might not fit in to the corporate world and therefore running my own business was a good idea.

The first business my dad had was retail: Frisby's Shoes shops. That was his first business, then he sold that. Obviously, there was a property side to that because I believe some of the shops were owned. I remember going to visit a development of his when I was small and being fascinated by it. In those days, tax was very high, so you pretty much had to reinvest rather than declaring any profit because otherwise it would just get taxed, so he invested in land and then built on it. It was quite a big development. So, he did do some property investing and owned the odd shop which he let out. He touched on it occasionally, though I wasn't at that point in time thinking that property was the way forward. In my early days, it was more a case of me thinking I should run a business. That's probably why I turned my property investing into what I would call more of a property business. Now, I employ people to help me run my property business and investing.

What did you study at university and what happened afterwards?

I studied business studies, which was driven by the fact that I was thinking, "Right, one day I want to run a business." The course also had a placement, which meant that I would work. You take a year out and work for a year in industry and I thought that would help me to find a job.

I graduated when there was a recession, so it was quite hard to find a job. I had to climb my way up the ladder, literally, because I got one job and it didn't last very long, then I had to get another. Neither of these were amazing jobs (one was in marketing, one was doing a little bit of analysis) and then I saw a job at Guinness advertised in the newspaper and applied and got it. That gave me a leg up because it was a nice big corporate company with good training: it was going places and there was a bit of a revolution going on there.

That shaped me in terms of my business career because I saw innovative things going on there. They were great people to work with, as well – a lot of my colleagues who were there at the start have gone on to do some amazing things.

I really enjoyed working there for a number of years. Then they were doing a bit of a merger and talking about moving location and I got asked to work for Unilever, which was close to where I lived. I wasn't quite sure what was happening with Guinness and Diageo and suspected that the business might move far away from where I lived. So I moved into Unilever and then went on from there, really.

What made you shift into property? Was it a gradual process or a sudden decision?

It was a very gradual process. People would say, "Oh, property is a good thing to get into." But when I was in my twenties, I had no idea about property investing. I was always fascinated by property and by then I'd bought my own house and I could see that was going up in value. I thought, "Well, there has to be something here, as other people are doing it." I'd get the paper through the door with all the properties for sale and I used to enjoy looking at it. Partly because I would be dreaming about what kind of nice house I might end up with one day, partly because I was thinking, "Gosh, I wish I could invest in another property." I went along to the Property Investor Show, then went on a course to learn more and that gave me the education, answering my questions such as "How do I get into it?" and "How can I pay for it?" I didn't even know there were such things as buy-to-let mortgages, or anything like that.

I read a lot of books and educated myself and that made a huge, huge difference and I thought, "Well, I'm just going to get on and follow what I've been taught." So I started buying a few properties.

This was alongside my job. Of course, the only constant in these big organisations is change. They were constantly changing. I was getting frustrated with my job and then there came an opportunity to leave, and so I did.

It gave me a little bit of time and breathing space because there was some money to carry on. I thought, "Well, I need to make this work. I'll do this for a certain amount of time and if it doesn't work I'll go and look for a job." I still haven't gone and looked for a job yet, so it seems to be going okay! That was about 12 years ago.

What are the main areas of your business and how has it evolved over time?

I have three main areas. Firstly, the area of buying property. I tend to buy property, renovate it, maybe change planning status, and then refinance and keep hold of it. Occasionally, I sell or develop properties, but normally I keep hold of them and add the income into my property portfolio.

I'm mainly an investor for income. In the early days, I wasn't so much but when the credit crunch came along that became a priority because I realised that the capital values that everybody said would be going up weren't. Finance was hard, so income had to be the key thing and then everything else was a bit of a bonus. Since then, I've geared myself around finding, or getting, high-income properties. I do a lot of HMOs currently. I used to do quite a lot of social housing for a while, which used to give me a significant income. So that's the property investment side.

Second, I have the lettings side of the business. Because I started to have so many properties, I got people in to help me manage them and then it started to make sense to manage other people's properties as well. So, I've established a lettings agency and we manage other people's properties too. I didn't do this initially, but now I'm pushing that and establishing a nice, large, lettings agency in the areas in which I invest. That's a growing area of business moving forward.

Third, there is consulting and mentoring. Early on I was asked to give presentations because I was considered someone who'd actually got on and made a success at the things that I'd learnt, such as how to deal directly with vendors. I've used various strategies over time, and bought a lot of properties by leafleting and finding people who are interested in selling their house fast. I used to come in, buy fast, and get a good deal. They needed to sell quickly, whether they were being repossessed or they had other reasons why they didn't want to put their house on the market. They would come direct to me.

So, I used to talk about that and then moved into social housing when the whole credit crunch came along. That was quite innovative at the time. People wanted to know more about what I was doing, how I was doing it, and what needed to be put in place. They were aware of the legislation, but they didn't know how to make it happen. I made it happen and then taught other people how to do the same. So, the third arm to my business is consulting and mentoring. I help other people out, which I enjoy. Sometimes it's through courses but more often through one-to-one mentoring: helping other people to copy my strategies in order to get involved in property.

Why do people choose you over your competitors?

At the moment, many people are coming to me for help and support in two main areas. One is to try and work out their strategy: "I want to get going. What should I do? How should I do it?" I'm quite good at helping people set their goals and work out what they need to do to get there. I find that some people head off in property and do something that doesn't really fit with their goals. They come into property because they want a better life: they want a bit of independence; they want some extra money; they want to go on holiday. Yet they'll often try to copy what I've done, which is create a property business – and you're then replacing one job with another and ending up working full-time again. I find that most people actually don't want that at all. They just want a few properties to give them a nice income with an agent to manage it, which gives them the freedom to go on and do something else with their time. They've got the luxury to do that. So, I help them formulate what kind of property investing they want to do, find out why they're doing it, and then help them create a plan to get there. One of the things is really to help people get going: identify what they want and their first steps, keep them going, keep them motivated when it's hard. I help to give them much more clarity as to what they should be doing. There are so many strategies out there that sometimes people get confused and try to jump around too much. I stop them bouncing around and get them focused because clarity is what helps people become successful.

Then the other area is high-income strategies. Once people have decided that they want to do high-income strategies, they often come to me – particularly for HMOs, as I'm doing a lot of those at the moment. A couple of years ago, I really focused on expanding my HMO portfolio and added over 100 rooms to my portfolio. So, I've really systemised the way of buying HMOs: adding some value through gaining planning permission, refurbishing, and then refinancing. Today, I take people round my properties, so they can see what's going on. I also help educate them on financing. The financing side is critical because it might be easy to buy one HMO when you've got a bit of money or can release some equity out of your own property that you live in, but generally that's only enough to buy one. If you don't understand how to recycle your cash, you can't keep going. So understanding this is critical. I help people understand how to value HMOs and how the banks see commercial valuations. I do an afternoon on that with my broker, which is quite a popular event.

You work on investment deals between £300k and £3 million. Which areas do you focus on in the UK?

I live in Surrey, so my main investment area is up and down the A3. It's West London and down towards the coast: the Guildford/Surrey area and the south coast, mainly around Portsmouth. I've been as far across as Bournemouth. I have a core area and then I will go outside of that a little. In my early days, if people gave me a deal I would almost always do it.

Looking back, I probably shouldn't have done, but at that point in time I was just keen to expand my portfolio. We'd almost buy properties anywhere if a good deal came along. So, I'm pruning some of those properties at the moment. Part of the tax changes are incentivising me to get rid of properties that are slightly out of my zone – which is off my current strategy.

What are the main challenges you've had over the years that you've learned from?

Every property I find provides its own challenge. One of the things I think I'm good at is not getting too put off by challenges and finding a way through any problem that comes my way. My most significant challenges have been on development projects. At one point I had a development project that the builder went bust on, so that cost me a lot of money. I think he knew he was going bust and cut many corners, so I had to undo a lot of the things he did and redo them. So, I've had my own nightmares that have provided challenges. That was when I was fairly experienced as well, so these things can happen at any stage. It's about how you deal with it that matters. Fortunately, I managed to get through it and work out what to do as I got some trusted contacts who helped me to get it finished. I used the network I've built up over time to help me.

It's important to have supportive people around you: experts, such as people to come in and survey the building, tell me what went wrong and what needed doing. There was asbestos, so I had to replace the roof as the original builder had not put down the right materials. I got a structural guy in to develop a report and a new builder had to come in to redo it all as it wouldn't have passed building control. Then, obviously, I needed a little more money than I first anticipated. So, you need to know how you can raise funds in order to do that. If you're doing everything on a shoestring budget, this is where you can come unstuck. I always say to people: be in a position to understand what happens if something goes wrong. What can you do and how can you mitigate your risks as much as possible?

I think a lot of people look at me because I've been in property a while, and think, "Oh, it must be easy for him." But it's not like that. I find that it's a constant battle to get things over the line with everything to do with property, especially around the finance side. You have to be persistent, so the challenge is consistency and persistency to actually make things happen. You need to stay focused, and do it with a smile on your face, otherwise you won't survive. You come across hurdles and you need to think around those hurdles to actually get things done and rally your team – whether it's your virtual team, your solicitors, your brokers, your banks, your letting agents, your builders – you have to get everyone in your team on board, so that when you have some issues along the way, you are all working together for a common cause.

For me, the challenges have just been constant and I've had to overcome them. For example, I've had banks not lend when I'm expecting them to lend, I've had the finance not being there when I needed it – all these types of issues. There isn't one single thing that I think, "Oh gosh, that was a massive challenge" because I am faced with issues every day. You are always going to be faced with challenges: it's how you overcome those that makes you successful.

What are your greatest lightbulb moments?

I wish I'd picked up on the fact that income was key much earlier on. I kind of knew it, but I didn't really follow it. I was more interested in finding property that was below market value, refinancing, and moving on, and less fussed about how much money it was making every month. I've now got a lot more experience, so I know that you need to renovate properties every so many years. Therefore, you need to be earning quite a lot of money out of your properties because you need to set money aside for renovations later on. There's also maintenance that needs to be done. So, all these things are usually a little more expensive than you first anticipate.

If I go around and ask other landlords, they generally say the same thing: it costs a lot more to run an investment property than they anticipated. When they do a little analysis on a piece of paper, they think, "Oh, yeah. This is going to make loads of money." But it probably doesn't make as much money as they thought because they haven't accounted for all the costs that come out of the woodwork. So, investing for income if you're holding a property is a good idea: make sure you've got a good margin. It's harder to find these days because I think values have gone up and rents haven't gone up quite as much, which is why HMOs are so popular because they deliver a better income out of a property.

What has been your biggest success or achievement? What are you proudest of?

I like the fact that I've helped a lot of people along their property journeys. I've helped them get onto the property ladder or have taken them to the next level. Some of them have gone on to do some great things. That's always nice. I'm proud of playing a small part in seeing people develop and grow.

Personally, it's probably about turning my property investing into a business and employing people, and therefore not having to run everything myself. That's probably been the biggest success for me, I would say.

For me, a lot of the motivation is around freedom and being able to choose to do what I want when I want. Seeing other people get there as well has been hugely rewarding for me.

What advice would you give to newbies to property investing?

I would just say: educate yourself as to how it all works. Know what you want and start with the end in mind. Then stay focused on that. Don't let fear hold you back because many people can be held back by fear. A lot of people want the golden deal. They see people who have done some very good deals. Quite often, the deal wasn't anticipated to be like that when they went into it, but it turned into a fantastic deal – because they were in it, they were winning it, and something positive happened. So, my biggest advice would be to get clear about where you're trying to head and why you're doing it and don't be held back by fear. That fear is often driven by not having enough knowledge. Take the first step and then learn and take the next step. Then, learn some more and take the next step. And so on. That way, you'll do it securely and safely.

Everyone always says, "Oh, I wish I'd invested a long time ago before so-and-so happened" or "If only I'd invested in property 10 years ago, I'd be sorted now." Well, you can't wind the clock back, so the best time to start is now. Everyone has been worried, certainly in the last several years, ever since the crash. Well, the property market has grown over the last five years (depending on where you invested). You could have done very well. We don't know what's going to happen in the future but invest wisely. Understand the risks and make sure that you mitigate the risks.

People always say, "Oh my gosh, what happens if property prices go down?" If you're investing for the longer term, it doesn't matter what happens to your property in the short term – it's the longer term that counts, as long as you can pay your mortgage. Make sure that you're covering yourself, with space to spare in terms of being able to cover your mortgage with the rent that's coming in. There are always opportunities, so buy cleverly, get some built-in discount, add some value somewhere, maybe do a refurbishment in order to build some safety net into your investing – that's certainly what I do.

What are the top mistakes your see other people making?

I think people get lazy about doing due diligence and knowing and understanding their area. Certainly, one of the reasons why I think I can pick up opportunities is because I understand the area, so I understand if something is a good deal or not a good deal quite quickly. Many people buy from sourcers initially and that's what I did. However, it's important to do your own due diligence – don't rely on theirs. Have a good understanding and knowledge of the marketplace and where you're buying and have good relationships with the people that you're buying from.

Number two: don't underestimate the costs. I've already mentioned that a lot of people underestimate the cost of renovation. They also forget all the other little things, like if they're using finance, arrangement fees and surveys, and so on. People become very optimistic about their budgets – get realistic on that. Be as accurate as you can be. Sometimes people don't do deals because they put the worst-case scenario in, and then suddenly the deal doesn't work. If you've put in a safety margin – a high interest rate, high refurbishment cost, a low-end sale or a low-end value once you've developed – then sometimes deals won't work. That's where getting a good understanding of all of your numbers allows you to assess a deal accurately and see whether it is a good or a bad one.

Don't be scared by all the analysis that you do and get into paralysis and fail to do anything. Be clear on what you're trying to achieve. I find people are a bit wishy-washy about what they want to do, so again they don't know a good deal when they see one because they're not quite sure what they're looking for.

What keeps you getting out of bed in the mornings and ready for the next challenge?

I love learning new things. I love growing as an individual. I love a challenge. I hope that throughout my life I'm continuing to grow and develop. That's what drives me. One of the reasons I run my own business is for freedom, so as long as I feel as though I'm in control and have the freedom to do what I want, that's important to me. That's one of the reasons why I'm running my own business, although at times I've had to work very hard at it. It certainly makes me feel like I'm making all my own decisions, which is great.

Moving forwards I want to make a mark on the property scene. I want to provide good-quality customer service to the tenants. I've been doing a lot of HMOs recently, so that's driven me to look at the whole idea of what people are calling 'co-living'. I have some visions around that, where I want to try innovative new things in my business. So, at the moment I'm going through a period of researching what is out there in the marketplace. There are some very big co-living environments across Europe and a few have made it into the UK.

I'm interested in the concept of mixed-age living, where you've got elderly people living with younger people, all sharing their experiences and interacting. Sometimes older people may be a bit lonely if they live by themselves in normal communities, so it's about how to combat loneliness and create communities around co-living, which I think is a really interesting concept. I'm spending some time at the moment looking into and reviewing that, to see how the shape of affordable housing is moving in the future. What could happen, what could be there, and what impact can I make and how can I help with that? It's about really starting to think about the tenants as opposed to thinking about, "I just need to buy another investment house." That's not motivational for me any more. It's more about "how can I provide a better lifestyle for the people who are living within my properties?" So, there's been a slight switch in emphasis and that's driving me forward.

CRAIG RENNOLDS

"When I was fourteen, a teacher told my class that we would be lucky if we could become dustbin men when we grew up."

Job Title: Chartered Building Surveyor/Property Investor.

Personal Bio: Chartered surveyor and director covering the areas of Bristol, Bath, and the South Hams, providing Homebuyer Reports, building surveys, and private valuations. I also carry out mortgage valuations for some lenders. My other business is property investment in the Bristol area.

Qualifications: BSc MRICS.

Business: Rennolds Surveyors Ltd., Bristol-Lets (Acorn Developments).

Services: Residential surveys (both homebuyer and full building surveys) and bank valuations, short-term lets, student lets, and normal family lettings.

Contact:

T: 07773724549

E: craig@crsurveyors.co.uk

Websites:

www.crsurveyors.co.uk

www.bristol-lets.co.uk

♦ ♦ ♦

I had a normal working-class upbringing and I attended the local comprehensive school in South Bristol. Both my parents left school at around fourteen or fifteen to start working full-time.

Although I went to a comprehensive I was more academic than my friends or family and actually managed to get 'O' levels and entry onto an ONC course in mechanical engineering. No one else in my family had qualifications beyond school and I wanted to be the first to achieve this.

Nothing really stands out from my school years, apart from starting to ride motor bikes when I was about sixteen, but that all ended when I had a major accident.

My father was a builder, plasterer, and floor layer, so I guess I was always destined to go into property in some way. My father thought that engineering was one step up from what he did and would be a good career for me, so pushed me in that direction. In fact, I found engineering a little bit too precise and just not for me, so in the end I followed him and became a builder. I took an interest from an early age in his building work and projects and from the age of about fourteen I worked on site with him. I used to do labouring for him and various other things. So even though I was pushed in the direction of engineering, I wasn't a natural engineer. I didn't have that sort of mind – engineers are very analytical and precise, machining components to a very high tolerance. This was not for me.

Initially, I applied for an apprenticeship with Rolls Royce and British Aerospace, which were the main employers in Bristol. I went along for interviews and I was offered a job as a trainee draftsman for British Aerospace. But they wanted certain 'O' level qualifications, including maths and English and I had just started riding a moped before I took my exams and had quite a bad accident. I fractured my ankle and I suppose that had an effect. Anyway, I didn't get the qualification they wanted in maths so, although they'd offered me the trainee draftsmanship, I needed to go back to college to take further exams to get what they required. In the end, I didn't really enjoy what I was doing, so I left British Aerospace and did a few other administration jobs before settling on building and construction.

I worked for a number of years as a labourer on different building sites and did a course in plumbing. When I was about twenty-seven, I went off on a gap year and spent seven or eight months in Australia, thinking about what I really wanted to do and travelling around, mainly in Western Australia. I ended up working for a roofing contractor in Perth and thought, "This is really what I want to do," although I didn't know whether I wanted to be on the trade side of things. I thought maybe something like surveying or architectural work would suit me more.

Once I was back from Australia, I decided to go back to college to take a degree in building surveying, to be able to earn more money than just labouring or plumbing. I spoke to a chartered surveyor back in 1989 who explained this was a job where you could run your own business but he stressed that many surveyors have difficulty in passing the strict RICS tests to become chartered. I wanted to put my building knowledge to good use!

Most chartered surveyors come from private school backgrounds and I did find there is a divide within the industry. I would say the minority come from working-class backgrounds like mine. So, I applied for courses with various universities and got accepted in the University of the West of England, in Bristol.

Even though I was from a building background and I grew up in this environment, I still learned a lot of things from my degree course – mainly about the defects in buildings and the structural integrity of buildings, and what defects to look for in buildings – 'building pathology', it is termed. For example, you have to investigate the possible causes of foundation movement, which could be due to broken drains, settlement, or other things.

I also needed the qualification to become a member of the RICS, so it wasn't just a case of studying for a degree. I had to study for two more years afterwards to become chartered.

It was a little more drawn out than your standard academic study. I also learned a lot about mechanical services in buildings, project management, cost analysis, building structures, and various other disciplines. Although older than my contemporaries, I enjoyed the course and was very surprised when I passed the RICS exams and qualified as a chartered surveyor in 1999. One of the major things which always interested me at the time was studying old buildings and building conservation.

Working with listed buildings, and older buildings, is one of your specialities, isn't it?

Yes. We have one client in particular who buys property and invests in listed buildings in Bath – flats and so forth – and rents them out. I carried out a building survey for him on a Grade II listed building, a £1.5 million maisonette, which seems like an awful lot of money for a maisonette outside London.

As a result of my interest in properties like that and the type of work we've ended up doing, we've become more specialised in that field: conservation and building surveys on listed buildings.

I've always liked old buildings. I like the way they were put together, the grandeur, especially of Georgian buildings, and how the builders of the time overcame the problems with little mechanical aids, such as cranes, etc – for instance erecting large four- and five-storey buildings incorporating ornate stonework to the facades, which is typical of the architecture of cities such as Bath.

Builders of the time used lime plasters or renders to the walls. Because the walls were solid, this material allowed the walls to breathe and moisture to evaporate. One of the problems with modern building techniques is the application of materials such as Portland cement to render solid walls. Portland cement does not allow the evaporation process to take place, forcing moisture to the inside wall of the house, which causes damp issues within the property. I just recommend the use of traditional materials for old buildings and using the old techniques because, obviously, those techniques were used because they worked – they allowed the building to 'breathe' and moisture to evaporate out through the wall. I am also interested in the use of lead sheet to roofs and the traditional techniques of working the lead passed down through the years by experienced builders. The use of plaster mouldings to produce ornate cornice work between the wall and ceiling junctions not only gives a sense of history but has a practical application in hiding shrinkage cracking during the build process.

Tell me about your early steps into property.

I refurbished a property in Bristol with my father, which made very little money. It was in Westbury-on-Trym, in Bristol. We overspent – which sounds a bit ludicrous when your father's a builder – but the estate agent I was dealing with said, "If you want top dollar for this, it has to be done to a high spec." We were putting in granite worktops for the kitchen and an en suite for one of the bedrooms, etc. So, although the property sold for more than any property had ever gone for on that road – around £80,000 – the actual profit we made was about £2,000 or £3,000. It was a learning curve because I realised you don't really need to go to that level of specification if you're buying and selling property. You tend to go along with the guidelines of the estate agents because they're going to sell the property for you. I suppose they do this because it's very easy for them to sell the property if it's been done to a really high specification and they don't have to worry about how much profit it makes.

I later invested in a couple of flats in Clifton, Bristol, with my wife. One defining moment was when my wife's mother retired and arrived in our house after selling her property in France – we had to quickly find a large enough house to convert into flats so that she would have a place to live.

In around 1993 or 1994, my wife and I bought a couple of period flats in Clifton, which is the more select area of Bristol. We bought one property on Vyvyan Terrace and another in Caledonia Place. One of them we sold on and made some profit – a bit more profit than the previous project – and the other became our first buy-to-let. My wife was pregnant at the time, so we moved into a country cottage in Backwell and had this idyllic life. Or so we thought. We had student tenants and everything seemed very nice. Students rented the flat in Clifton for about three or four months – and then they disappeared, leaving us short of both our deposit and a few months' rent, which was a shock to the system and a baptism of fire into the investment market.

We were naïve at the time as to landlord–tenant relationships. We felt a bit burnt for a while and didn't do any more investing until around 2001, when we bought another property which was famously known as 'Sadly Broke' (Bradley Stoke).

It was going very cheaply but I said to my wife, "I really don't fancy investing in property out here" as I had got used to the old properties in Clifton! But she said, "Oh, I think we'll do well here." And she was right: we still own the property, we've just re-rented it, and the value's increased three times, to around £390,000. So, it's just getting your ducks in a row, as they say, and learning a way forward.

The learning curve was steep and we learned mostly through trial and error. We just looked in agents' windows to see what properties were renting for at the time.

We got into the property business more from necessity than anything else as we required a second income.

I didn't finish my degree until 1996, so I was still studying and working part-time for a local authority – it was all quite complicated and stressful because we also had quite a lot going on with our properties. I had no mentoring, as such, because I don't think there were many people at the time who invested in property, and very few training courses.

What were the main challenges that you faced along the way?

I don't think the buy-to-let mortgage had been created when we first started investing, so the big lesson was getting your finances right. Our bank manager at the time was quite understanding. He said, "Well, we've got a charge over this property, so we can lend you the money to buy another property." It was quite a learning curve with the finances. We got into a few sticky situations, though, and came close to being repossessed, and we had to borrow some money off the family. So, as well as picking the right tenants and getting the right contract in place, getting your finances sorted out and not stretching yourself too far was also important. Later on, it became easier because the buy-to-let mortgage was introduced, where you needed to only put down 10 to 15%. But at the time we were running our first couple of properties, we needed about 20 to 25% deposit.

Further along, we carried out more major extensions and loft conversions to properties and I managed the work myself, which was extremely stressful. For example, we refurbished and extended a Victorian semi-detached property, which involved removing a considerable amount of soil to the rear of the property and building a retaining wall with mainly manual labour due to access problems to the rear of the property. The cost was three times over our budget and we had to borrow at commercial rates to complete the project.

On several occasions, I felt like giving up – in fact, we did not invest at all between 1996 and 2001.

At the moment, the biggest obstacle for property investors and landlords is the changes in legislation and taxes applied to buy-to-lets. Although I have been a landlord now for sixteen years and invested in property so that I could create my own pension, due to government changes in taxation the profit margins to run the business are now small and I know many landlords who are selling their properties as the situation is no longer profitable. The private housing market is shrinking and although there is a greater need for housing, the government has made it very difficult for existing landlords to invest. This is a real shame.

Tell me about your business today.

I invest in various types of property with my wife, including a commercial unit let to an architects' practice. We have a medium-sized portfolio of properties or 'units', as some houses are split into flats.

I also run a surveying practice in the South West in which my wife is a co-director. We provide services such as homebuyer surveys and carry out mortgage valuation work for some lenders. As I am a building surveyor, I can also carry out building surveys and we are often required to do so. I cover the areas of Bristol, Bath, and South Hams in Devon, splitting my week between both areas.

We work for ourselves and mostly manage the rental properties ourselves.

We invest in various types of property but more recently have started using Airbnb for short lets, using cleaning contractors to service the units.

From the investment point of view, we've bought three or four properties at auction or after the auction. Some of them were already converted and we just refurbished them. One or two of the properties we have converted ourselves. Getting your costs correct is really important when you refurbish conversions. We try to get the builders' quotes set but builders have this habit of coming up with extras and saying, "Well, you didn't mention this in the original specification, so that's going to cost you more." So that was another big learning curve.

I should mention one particular person who, unfortunately, is now not with us. He died of cancer three or four years ago but at a later time in my investment career became my mentor. He had a publishing business in Bristol and invested in property on the side and ended up with a portfolio of about 125 units, so he was pretty successful. He worked everything on a numbers basis.

We attended a couple of auctions together and he'd say, "You need to really study the auction pack because there could be restrictions placed on certain properties," so we'd go through that together. Then he'd say, "Well, as long as the figures stack up, it works. Doesn't matter where it is." I don't quite agree with his philosophy on that because I think some of the properties we've got now we might have to get rid of because they are in areas where the local authorities are issuing selective licences, and there are complications attached to that. There's a lot of money involved in getting them to a standard that the local authorities are happy with.

In fact, at one of the first auctions I bid at, my friend was supposed to be there to give me moral support but couldn't make it.

In the end, I bid on a property which included a commercial unit below it, so we ventured – in a small way – into the commercial side of investing as well. On the surveying side, we'd started up a partnership with a company and dealt mainly with mortgage lenders and we'd get homebuyers and building surveys off the back of that. More recently, in the last couple of years, we've picked up direct instructions from a website called *reallymoving.com* and we're signed up with a few other internet-based companies where we just do the work, and they take a very small percentage, about 5 or 10%.

When we used to work with the smaller firms like Chancellors Associates, they would take around 30 to 40% of the fee, so we've moved away from that now.

So, you work mainly with people in Bristol, and South Hams in Devon, splitting your week between the two areas?

We still work in Bath and there we do tend to specialise in listed buildings because the majority of the buildings there are older. But we've also now surveyed older buildings, such as farm buildings and artisan buildings, like thatched buildings. You have to be open and consider whatever a client in that area is buying, really. It just depends on what work is available and who's buying what.

Tell me about the kind of people that you help.

The surveying business is set up to help homebuyers, people remortgaging or looking for equity release, private buyers who want us to look at a property with many defects and tell them whether these are possible defects or of no significance. Quite often, it's the case that people want some money discounted, so they'll say, "Well, we found certain defects in the property," and they want us to put a case forward for a price reduction. We also value for probate work, valuing property which may be contentious in probate.

On the investment side, we do short-term lets. We've been running a B&B for about 18 months, which is quite labour-intensive with the changing of beds and so on. We run student lets and traditional family lets, so we split our time between surveying and investments and obviously we try to help people who need rented accommodation.

We helped a lady recently who couldn't get through any of the agency credit checks so she came to us, directly, and we took a view on her situation. She seemed like a nice enough person. We checked out what we could through her employment and then offered her the property in Bradley Stoke. She was over the moon about that because her poor credit and the fact that she had a part-time job meant she couldn't go through the normal channels, with a letting agent.

We try to help people as much as we can but, obviously, you have to be careful. For instance, we tend not to let to council tenants simply because of issues around universal credit, like how difficult it is, sometimes, to obtain the rental income from the tenant.

I donate to cancer charities and intend to give more over time. This is mainly due to the fact I lost my father five years ago to prostate cancer and believe that money spent on research is vital.

What differentiates you from your competitors?

From the surveying point of view, we have testimonials on the website and up until now they're all five out of five ratings. I hope that they choose us based on the testimonials and, to a lesser extent, I suppose, on my background. In fact, I haven't really elaborated too much on my practical background on the website – maybe I should!

Customer service, obviously, plays a large part. For example, the fact that we tend to ring clients back after we've done the survey to give our initial thoughts. Other companies tend to just produce a kind of generalised survey, whereas we try to be more bespoke. We'll ask the client what their concerns are with the property before we go there, so we can tailor our service. That is what seems to come up in the testimonials. A couple of people have said the report was more detailed than they expected. They like the fact that we'd put a number of photographs into the homebuyer's report. We try to go the extra mile and produce something which people are happy with.

What are your top 'aha' moments over the years?

One such moment came when I finally became a chartered surveyor. It was a real struggle with a young baby at the time and no money! After struggling as a mature student, and with my wife's support, I managed to turn our financial situation around to our favour over the next five years!

I realised after buying a building with three flats and a commercial unit that title splitting increased the value of the property and allowed greater borrowing. As a purely income-producing stream, student lets work well and there is a benefit of having third-party guarantors. People may say that student lets are difficult but in my experience, students are great and generally look after the property.

The Airbnb unit that we have run has also worked extremely well and it allows us to meet diverse people who are visiting Bristol. We have had many visitors from abroad and have met many interesting individuals. Serviced accommodation has been given much better tax treatment and is regarded as a business, so does not fall under Section 24, loss of interest relief.

Top mistakes to avoid?

Investing in low-value units in deprived areas now attracts licensing and other expenses which has affected our profits.

It is unfortunate, but by local authorities increasing both regulation and the costs of licencing to combat the 'slum landlord', we have all been tarred with the same brush. Landlords who look after tenants properly have been punished and treated the same as a landlord who doesn't care about the well-being of a tenant or the property. This situation is causing landlords to sell and the local authorities will have even less private housing to house tenants who really are in need and, of course, rents will increase due to lack of supply.

The other mistake is not fully understanding the cost implications of refurbishment and the need to get the building specification as detailed as possible.

What are your top tips for newbies to property – what do you wish you'd known when you first started out?

If I was advising somebody purely about investing in property, the major consideration is that they know the local market in the area where they wish to invest, the infrastructure, bus routes, and things like that. Especially if you're dealing with student accommodation, the landlord needs to know how close the bus route is into college, how popular the area is with students, and the competition. Generally, I think, new investors need to know how good the infrastructure is, including rail links and bus routes, possible rental income, and, of course, profit. For instance, there's quite a big supermarket complex in Bradley Stoke, almost a city in itself. Knowing the market and researching the local market is essential.

I recommend carrying out research into rental demand, location of public services and infrastructure, property values, etc. Get expert advice on the structural stability of the building you want to buy and the defects it may have. Most importantly, understand how the finance is arranged based on rental income and value and understand what your financial commitment will be.

A quick checklist would be:

– Research the property market you want to invest in and location, and be aware of restrictions, such as planning restrictions on the development of HMOs in your area.

– Understand what defects may be hidden in any proposed property purchase and seek professional advice from a surveyor. This is vital in raising your awareness of possible costs in the future, which will affect your profit margins. Most properties will require a maintenance programme and money set aside to pay for repairs in the future.

– Seek advice on the value and rental potential/income of the property you wish to purchase – will the rental income meet lender criteria?

– Be aware of the effects of Section 24 and loss of interest relief on your profit and consider buying through a limited company. Seek advice from a property accountant.

– Consider building a foundation of HMO/student-let properties to give positive cash flow before moving on to more complex and larger projects, such as converting commercial premises to residential or mixed use.

From a surveying point of view, I would say potential investors/property buyers need to understand or get the advice of a surveyor to know what the possible defects are in a property and whether the property is structurally sound and stable. Also, I think one of the biggest concerns for lenders concerning property investment now is Section 24 – the loss of interest relief on mortgage loans and so forth – which impacts your profitability and your portfolio. Therefore, existing landlords will come under scrutiny from lenders concerning existing properties owned – 'stress testing'.

If you're setting up a property investment business, you could also look at setting up a foundation through purchasing HMOs or student lets to provide you with the cash flow that you need before moving into other fields or more complex projects. And, of course, there are other issues when you buy property now: there's an increased stamp duty on second homes and other things to be aware of that have cost implications. I personally think that it's a little bit more difficult from a cost point of view, and because of the restrictions placed upon the private-rented sector, to develop a property portfolio now than it was eight to ten years ago.

Having said that, I think it's still quite possible, if you're determined, to build a property portfolio – I wouldn't say easily but it can be done and you can become, as they say on property courses, financially independent.

Tell me about your biggest successes or achievements.

My biggest achievement has been building a successful property business with a positive cash flow which has given us financial independence. Becoming a chartered surveyor at the ripe age of 33 has been a major achievement, especially for someone with my background!

I am also proud of the very good feedback we have had from our clients for the surveying business. I have also expanded into the South Hams area and we are intending to buy property here in the future.

I am particularly proud of our achievements in property, that is, the properties we have invested in and the refurbishment work we have carried out. I am also proud of overcoming the problems faced with the property crash of 2008/9 where some of my friends and company owners were made bankrupt.

From the surveying point of view, I'm pleased with the way the business has expanded and moved away from relying on third parties, such as Chancellors Associates. Now, we answer directly to the client without suffering introduction fees!

Because I went into surveying at a relatively late age, that has been a major achievement for me from an academic point of view and a business point of view as well. Also, I'm proud of the fact that we managed to develop the business not just in Bristol and Bath but also in the South Hams.

My wife and I share a passion for houses and their repairs! We work together both in surveying and as landlords, which has entitled us to share many experiences. Some partners would not be able to work together as we have done and we are a team in that sense.

At my comprehensive school in Bristol, when I was fourteen, a teacher told my class that we would be lucky if we could become dustbin men when we grew up. To that teacher, I would like to say, "There is no way you should restrict what people want to be at such an early age." I think that statement made me so angry that I had to prove to myself and my family how wrong this attitude is in the modern world! I have tried very hard with my own children to empower them with self-belief so that they can study and expand their knowledge in what they are interested in – always conscious not to narrow or close any doors for the future.

DEEPAK SINGH UDASSI

"For every pound that a client has spent on their loft, they've earned £10 back on the value increase. It's nuts."

Job Title: Managing Director, City Lofts London.

Personal Bio: Multi award-winning loft conversion specialist, based in London. Also, a Property Certification Specialist – providing property certificates for agents, landlords and home owners.

Business: City Lofts London.

Services: Award-winning luxury loft conversions. Expertise and master craftsmanship collected over 27 years of building experience. Creating more living space within the home and increasing the value of your property. Pioneers of a new breed of builder that puts the customer first at every turn.

Certifications and Awards

2017: Winner. FMB London Master Builder Of The Year.
2017: Best Service Award, Houzz.
2017: Engineering & Construction Awards, best luxury lofts.
2016: BUILD Engineering & Construction Awards, best loft conversion winner.
2015: Best Service Award, Houzz.
2012 & 2014: FMB Master Builder nominees.

Contact:

T: 0845 519 4321

E: info@cityloftslondon.com

Website: www.CityLoftsLondon.com

◆ ◆ ◆

I was brought up in West London, so I am a born and bred Londoner. I then studied for a master's degree in management systems at City University.

At university, I had a deep interest in and around property, and I always felt that I would somehow go down that route after my academic education. My academia took me through to the age of 22, when I completed my Masters. Following that, it was straight into the graduate training programme at Centrica, which was a two-year stint in industry. That was good fun and pretty cool.

In my particular intake there were about 8,000 applicants for 19 roles, so it was like Dragons' Den to get in. I always wanted to do a two or three-year stint in industry to flex that muscle, as it were, before I leapt into property.

I should add that throughout my academic and career training, I retained the services of a mentor. He was a chap called Professor Eric Mooman OBE, who has recently passed away, and he helped me to set my sights higher. He was my marketing professor at university.

I continued to work with him on several marketing projects post qualification, and he always helped me aspire to more. He opened a lot of doors for me, which was very useful. He was actually an MP for about 30 years before he retired.

How did you get started in property?

I always had one eye on property, so I knew that was what I was going to go into. At that period in time, about 2004 or 2005, property was everything. The demand was so hot and every man and his dog was turning their hand to property. The Sarah Beeney show didn't really help things, where everyone thought they could get in, make a quick buck, and get out again. It was very much the kind of music at the time and I was no different. I completed my two-year contract at Centrica in 2006 and then dived into property. But then, of course, the world economic crash happened, which meant that it was much harder to get people to part with their money.

The trajectory to where we are now is as follows. We started off doing property maintenance and professional property certification works. At our peak, we had about 75 London estate agents as our clients. We were doing lots of certification and maintenance work for them. The natural progression from there was that more maintenance led to bigger construction work. From there, we found ourselves taking on quite big projects, typically quarter-of-a-million-pound refurbs.

We really were climbing up the property ladder in its truest sense. The challenge though was scalability, and it was a challenge because a residential construction business is nigh on impossible to scale unless you specialise. One day we were fitting a kitchen or a bathroom, the next day refurbing a grade II listed property in prime central London. These are very, very different skill-sets.

You may think that would make it more lucrative but not so, because with one-off big construction projects, you're putting all your resources in one basket. So, when other opportunities do come along, you're then having to break up teams to take on other work, and that lowers productivity on the current project. This is why you so often hear the complaint that "The builder let me down. I can't get hold of him. He promised one thing and then did something else." All these things come down to small firms, be it a one-man band or a small company, who are unable to meet expectations because they do not have the people, the processes or the systems with which to take on more work in a sustainable way.

Therefore, in 2010, we took the decision to specialise in lofts. What we wanted to do was be the absolute undisputed best in one thing and to be known for that one thing only, and for that we chose loft conversions. We chose lofts because we deemed that to be the most scalable form of residential construction work.

That was a real fork in the road moment for us when we decided to specialise. That's where things started to shoot off in the right direction.

Why are lofts the most scalable form of residential construction work – rather than, say, kitchen or bathroom renovations?

This is because things like kitchens and bathrooms are supply-led – people don't go out looking for a kitchen fitter. They first go out looking for a kitchen, then they worry about who's going to fit it after that.

Everything was aligned in terms of the economic background. The social background was set with people needing more space. London is a relatively small city and it's over populated. The population is growing but new house builds are not keeping pace. There is a pent-up stress in the housing market for more space. We've got kids going to Uni now, being sold the dream, but not getting a graduate job at the end of it and then moving straight back home with their parents –the boomerang generation of kids. After three years of independence, coming back home to their childhood bedroom is a bit of a grind. So, there are some big reasons why people need more space.

The divorce rate has never been higher than it has been now; we're talking close to 50%. This also feeds into creating a demand for more space. At the same time, you've got more babies being born. There are numerous valid reasons why people need to build up into their loft. Also, the stamp duty has increased, which means that it's become less viable for people to move to a bigger property and more viable for them to make their current homes better in order to get the space that they need.

There's the additional point that the London housing market is such that one lick of paint is going to increase the property value, so imagine what happens when you get the loft done. We've had situations where we're working in prime parts of town, such as Fulham, where for every pound that a client has spent on their loft, they've earned £10 back on the value increase. It's nuts.

What are your specialisms? Why would someone come to you rather than a competitor?

Since we took the decision to specialise in lofts, things have gone from strength to strength. We've picked up more awards than we literally know what to do with. We're talking customer service awards from Houzz, which is the biggest interior design platform on the planet. We've won the Best of Houzz three out of four years in a row. We've won the BUILD Construction and Engineering awards two years in a row and probably the pinnacle has been 2017. Just last year, we won the Federation of Master

Builders' London Master Builder Award. That has been the most significant one; that has really opened doors for us. We're now regularly asked to attend policy briefings with shadow ministers and ministers to advise on the challenges that small building companies face and solutions to those problems from our perspective. We're regularly wheeled out to policy makers representing industry at policy level.

Who is your typical client?

Our typical demographic of client would be aged between 35 and 65; working professionals, very often with a keen eye on design. We're not the average builder, so we have design-led clients. We're not just here to build lofts and our clients understand that. We're here to create a little bit more into that space and add luxury to people's homes. We've got a clear mantra in the business: if you're doing the loft, you want to do it well.

The average age of the first-time buyer now, as far as I'm aware, is 37 years old and that's increasing. London and the UK have got an issue where you've got fully-grown adult kids still living in the family home, which is not ideal for everyone. It's not ideal for the parents and it's not ideal for the kids.

Really, all they can do as a stop-gap solution is either move to a bigger home, which is unfeasible at the moment because of the stamp duty changes (meaning that it's costing a lot more to move), or, the obvious solution, spend the money instead on extending into the loft space, giving an extra bedroom, a bathroom, a break-out space. This solves the problem of not having the space and at the same time increases the value of the home, so it really is a no-brainer to get these things done.

You've also got multi-generational homes nowadays – that's another big one. There are working professionals who are taking care of their kids and, on the other end of the spectrum, they are also taking care of their elderly parents.

This is another big reason why people come to us. Probably the biggest reason is growing families: the 2.4 family which is looking to move home but simply cannot afford to, so they develop the loft instead.

We generally work on homes within the M25. But we will stretch out to the bordering Home Counties, where required. Greater London is my local stomping ground, but we'll also go to areas further afield. We're talking maybe Barnet, South Bucks, Berkshire; the kind of wider areas across London.

We're growing very, very rapidly. We've recently moved HQ to South-West London. Our design centre is in Hampton Wick now, and this is proving a very useful base from which to expand further. The team is growing very quickly. The level of work we're turning around volume-wise is increasing also.

Is there as much demand for lofts outside London?

There's any number of reasons why a home owner or a household would need more space and our challenge is to solve their problem. Let's say that you had two neighbours who came to us, at the exact same time, and they wanted the exact same loft. Mr and Mrs Smith wanted to increase the value of the home purely and simply and that was their motivation. But Mr and Mrs Jones, next door, needed the space because they've got baby number three on the way. Even though they're both getting the same loft, at the exact same time, every single micro-decision that they make from the time that they come to us to the time that we put the completion certificate in their hand will mean that they're going to have two very different lofts at the end of it. This is because everyone has a different budget. We need to make sure that their budget is used as sensibly as it can be to solve their problem, be it increasing value or giving them the most usable space and maximum utility for their growing family.

What sort of challenges do you face day to day?

To give you an example, we had a client who bought a property with a shockingly illegally converted loft. It was very shoddily done by a bunch of cowboys. That illegal conversion has caused structural havoc on the rest of the house. For example, moving walls, warped floors, doors that don't now open because doorways have warped out of shape. It was so poorly converted that it even had cracked joists. The structural problems were enormous, and the home was a death trap.

The client came to us very humbly and said, "I'd like a loft." Simply, "I'd like a loft." Now, when we went there to carry out our survey, we discovered that there was a massive problem. Then, we dug a bit deeper and the back story came out of what had happened. The structural issues hadn't been picked up by the solicitors upon purchase and they hadn't been picked up by the surveyors who carried out the valuation. This guy, with a young family, has been working his whole life so that he can buy his first ever home in the UK, and they've bought themselves a lemon. A complete lemon.

When I went there, the bloke was in pieces. At the end of my survey, I put my hand on his shoulder and said, "One way or another, we will fix your home and allow your family to move back in." At that point, the bloke broke down in tears.

We're having to do a lot of remedial work, not only the loft but other structural fixing around the house. But, we never forget that these are people's homes, and these are people's lives.

So, the moment I go in to see a client, I've got a duty of care to give them the absolute best that I can possibly give. Now, that might mean things that they don't want to hear such as how much things are going to cost to fix. If I've identified a problem, then I feel that I've got a duty of care to carry it out. We are now in the process of actually getting this guys life back on track by fixing the dodgy work that the cowboys have done before us.

We're currently completing about 40 or 50 lofts a year. Every client has got a story. This one is at the front of my mind because we're working on it right now.

What lessons have you learned over the years?

Just be very careful who you decide to go into business with. We've certainly learnt the hard way where we've had less-than-perfect business associates that we've worked with, whose integrity wasn't to the same level as ours. Pick your partners well. There's no substitute for trust in a business.

But every cloud has a silver lining and it's important to mention that City Lofts is run by two of us. My business partner's name is Kulveer Sanghera. Kulveer is a building maestro. There's nothing that he couldn't build and there's no problem that he can't solve. That, coupled with my ability to find the ideal solution, within budget, for a customer's problem by way of adding space to their home, means that what we're really doing is changing the paradigm of small London builders.

I've been friends with Kulveer since the age of 11. It helps that we've been kind of living in each other's pockets since we were children. What's very nice is one always dreams of building a business with your best pal and when you do it, it means that you get to share the problems and share the fun times. As long as you can make every day a bit of a laugh, it's perfect. It's really good.

We're raising the bar, and people are now coming to expect a higher level of service from their contractors. Service is everything. If you take service away from the equation, you're not left with much.

What do I mean by service?

Service, effectively, is talking. It's a two-way, ongoing chat with your homeowner to understand what they need and, at the same time, giving them the best of your expertise. If you put those things together from day one and you continue talking, it is inevitable that the client will walk up those stairs to their new loft and fall in love with the space that's been created. That's what true service is.

What were your main 'aha' moments throughout your career?

The lightbulb moment, you could call it, was when we got up from our side of the table and walked around to the other side and put ourselves in the customers' shoes. It was the moment when we said, "Right. If I was the customer what would I like to hear, what would I like to see, what would I like to receive from my builder?" The moment we did that, we then reverse engineered our whole building and design process to wrap around our customers' needs. It was a question of taking our process apart and putting it back together again purely with the aim of seeing things from the customers' perspective. As a result, it means that we deliver superb craftsmanship coupled with unrivalled service.

What are you proudest of achieving?

Kulveer and I are both Sikh, so charity is a big part of our upbringing. As a business, we fully support several charities, in particular one called Educate To Save (you can find out more at www.educatetosave.com), where we are now sponsoring several poverty-stricken children through a full education programme over in India. I'm on the executive committee for that charity, so we're always beating the drum for them.

The thing I'm proudest of achieving in a professional capacity is serving those clients who otherwise we know would not have received the same level of service if they went anywhere else.

However, the only thing that really matters is the kind of selfless work that we do outside of building lofts. Lofts are great fun; it's really a superb industry when you rise above the detritus. But even so, the only legacy that really matters when you shuffle off this mortal coil, as it were, is the selfless work that you've left behind. This is why charity is a big part of what we do.

What advice do you have for others wanting to achieve what you have?

My advice would be: for every bit of success that you achieve, give something back.

www.PowerhousePublishing.com

.

www.ingramcontent.com/pod-product-compliance
Lightning Source LLC
LaVergne TN
LVHW051232080426
835513LV00016B/1538